Selected Works

Selected Works of Yi Ok

By Yi Ok

Translated by
Won-Chung Kim
Christopher Merrill
Hyeonwu Lee

Homa & Sekey Books
Paramus, New Jersey

FIRST EDITION

Copyright © 2024 by Homa & Sekey Books
English translation copyright © 2024 by Won-Chung Kim, Christopher Merrill, and Hyeonwu Lee
Cover art: Chae Jongki

All rights reserved. No part of this book may be reproduced, stored in a retrieval system, or transmitted in any form, or by any means, electronic, mechanical, photocopying, recording or otherwise, without prior permission from the publisher.

Library of Congress Cataloging-in-Publication Data

Names: Yi, Ok, 1760-1815, author. | Kim, Won-Chung, 1959- translator. | Merrill, Christopher, 1957- translator. | Lee, Hyeonwu, 1958- translator.
Title: Selected works of Yi Ok / by Yi Ok ; translated by Won-Chung Kim, Christopher Merrill, Hyeonwu Lee.
Description: First edition. | Paramus, New Jersey: Homa & Sekey Books, 2024.
Identifiers: LCCN 2024002021 | ISBN 9781622461196 (paperback)
Subjects: LCSH: Yi, Ok, 1760-1815--Translations into English. | LCGFT: Poetry. | Short stories.
Classification: LCC PL989.9.O4 S45 2024
LC record available at https://lccn.loc.gov/2024002021

Published by Homa & Sekey Books
3rd Floor, North Tower
Mack-Cali Center III
140 E. Ridgewood Ave.
Paramus, NJ 07652

Tel: 201-261-8810, 800-870-HOMA
Fax: 201-261-8890
Email: info@homabooks.com
Website: www.homabooks.com

Printed in the USA
1 3 5 7 9 10 8 6 4 2

Acknowledgements

This work was supported by the English Translation of 100 Korean Classics program through the Ministry of Education of the Republic of Korea and the Korean Studies Promotion Service of the Academy of Korean Studies (AKS-2016-KCL-1230003).

Contents

Acknowledgements	/ v
Introduction	/ 001
Short Odes of Kyŏnggŭm	/ 015
Plain Verses	/ 071
Stories	/ 107
About the Translators	/ 137

Introduction to the Works of Yi Ok

Prologue

Yi Ok (1760-1815) wrote during an unprecedented era of transition, which was marked by the last monarchal reforms in the history of the Chosŏn dynasty. Eminent scholars of the practical learning known as Sihak, like Yŏnam Pak Chiwŏn (1737-1805) and Tasan Chŏng Yakyong (1762-1836), took the lead in calling for social reform and changes in the way of thinking. The introduction of Catholicism, a Western religion, threatened the traditional order, which was based on Confucianism. A society forged by noblemen or yangban disintegrated, undone by the negative effects of the civil service examination, while middle- and lower-class accumulation of wealth led them to demand more. The downfall of the aristocracy and the rise of the lower classes shook the feudal society, posing not only a crisis in the reformation of the dynastic system but also an opportunity. If the shifts in Chosŏn society resembled those in France pre- and post-Revolution, its dénouement was much different. The enthusiasm for change did not create a virtuous circle but soon gave way to inertia, and royal authority suffered a precipitous decline, with some royal families controlling the government, blocking social and cultural development. The Chosŏn dynasty failed to seize its opportunity.

But revolutionary change was afoot in the literary world. Writers attempted to incorporate new ideas in their work, refusing to stick with old stylistic ways, the most conspicuous change being the composition of essays on minor subjects (sop'ummun 小品文). Confucian intellectuals traditionally wrote in an elegant ancient style. But in this era, short narratives concerning one's feelings and daily affairs composed in a free style, sop'ummun, became popular. King Chŏngjo regarded this form of writing evil and ordered a rectification of literary style (文體反正).

Yi Ok was the sacrificial lamb of this campaign. When Yŏnam Pak Chiwŏn wrote *A Diary of the Je-ho River* in the style of sop'ummun, he was reprimanded. But Yi was ordered into military service, a kind of banishment the nobility was exempted from. He was the only writer to receive this punishment for composing sop'ummun. Nor did he cease writing in this way. His essays on minor subjects reveal his nuanced language, compassionate bearing, and unique perception of things. Yi creates his own unique universe in his essays better than any of his contemporaries. In this sense he was in the vanguard of a changing literature.

It was not long before Yi Ok's existence and writings became known to the world, though he was not a civil officer, and his works were never anthologized. His writings survived because Kim Ryŏ (1766-1822), his friend and classmate at the royal academy (Sŏnggyun'gwan), collected his posthumous works in *The Complete Writings of Kim Ryŏ, Tamjŏng Ch'ongsŏ*, which came to be known relatively later. Some of Yi's writings were also scattered in university libraries. All his works were collected and translated by the Silsahaksa Association of Classical Literature and published as *Complete Works of Yi Ok* in 2009 by the Humanist Press. Finally, readers can see Yi Ok's body of work in its entirety. His writings continue to be beams of light in dark times.

Yi Ok's Life and Works

Yi's other name was Kisang, his penname was Munmuja, and he had several other pennames, including Maehwaoesa. He was a descendant of Prince Hyoryŏng, King Sejong's elder brother, who had a keen interest in Buddhism. Though his family descended from royalty, his direct ancestor was the offspring of a concubine. His great-great-grandfather's military service to the nation had been distinguished, and so he was considered to be a nobleman from a concubine line of the family, which meant he could take the examination for government office. His family had lived for generations in Namyang, a western sea town in Kyŏnggi Province, acquiring enough wealth for him to live there comfortably.

Little is known about Yi's childhood. He left no records, and no chronology of his life has survived. His name first appears in *The Annals* when he was in his early 30s, preparing for higher examination as a student at Sŏnggyun'gwan, when King Chŏngjo reprimanded him for writing essays on minor subjects. Many were warned not to write sop'ummun, but Yi's case was more serious because he was a Confucian scholar at Sŏnggyun'gwan (the most important higher educational institution in Korea, founded in Seoul in 992). Descendants of cabinet officers or eminent families could escape punishment, but Yi had no connections; hence a second reprimand condemned him to military service, which noblemen were ordinarily exempt from, a punishment he suffered not once but twice.

He abandoned the civil service exam for government service and returned home. But his stint in the capital became the main source of his writing, for he had read many books there, experienced daily life, and observed the ways of the world. His military service also provided him with material for his writings, serving in the Chŏngsan district, Ch'ungch'ŏng province (currently Ch'ŏngyang) and Samga district, Kyŏngsang province (Sach'ŏn), the only places he visited except Seoul. His life and experience of local culture in these districts contributed to the idiosyncratic nature of his work.

After returning home, he worked during the day and studied at night, writing about his personal life: how he made fishing grounds by damming the sea, cultivated millet fields, and supervised the transportation of grain from his fields. Nature, animals, plants, farm produce, livestock—these became his main literary subjects and companions in his later life, when he conversed with nature. No account survives of his death. His life was quite humble, for a Confucian intellectual.

The record of his life is fragmentary, and his writings closely track those fragments. His works can be classified into three periods: his preparations for the civil service examination, his military service, and his return home. During the first period, he wrote many prose poems, a literary form called pu (賦) which falls between verse and prose, in which he boasted of his writing skills. Because pu was an examination subject in the Chosŏn dynasty, all students practiced writing pu, and most of Yi's prose poems date from his years at Sŏnggyun'gwan. His pu writing was different from others, who usually wrote one or two pieces perfunctorily. I will treat this point at greater length below.

Sŏnggyun'gwan gave Yi opportunities to observe changes in society in Seoul and ways of living, notably among the lower classes within and without the Fortress of Seoul, about whom he wrote several works. Seoul Fortress was not only the center of Chosŏn dynasty politics but also a space where products from around the country were traded. A market grew up around Chongno, which was crowded with merchants buying and selling, inspiring new forms of entertainment, like musical troupes and book-reading storytellers. Many literary works depict the rise of this new culture in the market, but Yi's works are different from those of other writers.

Consider "The Swindler at the Market," which concerns a merchant who cheats and steals from a country bumpkin and sells forgeries. Why depict a criminal, a heretofore unprecedented character in literature? Yi wanted to correct this habitual fraudster, though he believed that such fraudsters were part and parcel of a vigorous commercial setting. Yi intended to faithfully portray the dynamics of this market through the swindler's reprehensible conduct.

"A Righteous Gisaeng" portrays the most famous gisaeng in Seoul. Numerous men of wealth and fame made desperate attempts to win her over—in vain. For she had her own man whom she loved with all her heart. When he was exiled to Cheju Island, she immediately sold her household goods to follow him. On Cheju Island, she treated him to luxurious food and drink, and after feasting and drinking every day they died together. Yi's portrait of this gisaeng was unprecedented in the history of the Chosŏn dynasty. Her behavior was shocking, and other writers might have depicted her in the rudest terms. But Yi regarded her as a righteous woman who did not hesitate to sacrifice her life for her beloved. Yi had discovered a new type of woman in the brighter corners of the capital.

"Songs of Namhak" features an ugly singer whose voice was very beautiful. Demand for music was high, and string ensembles (chulp'ungnyu), which resembled Western chamber orchestras, performed in the market and houses of the nobility. Namhak came from the lower classes to make a living by singing. The unique tone of his voice was beautiful enough to be called the voice of heaven, and because he was a countertenor he could sing woman's parts. No one listening to him could help but shed tears. Yet he dared not show his face to the audience, singing behind a screen. Yi's affection for this ill-starred man gives the impression that it is for him a kind of self-portrait.

Yi captured a changing world by portraying the lives of eccentrics in his own peculiar way, cultivating a style of writing that was unacceptable to his Confucian society and to King Chŏngjo, who censured his writing as "disrespectful and bizarre." But his downfall was a product not only of his style but of his affection for the people he portrayed—and lack of supporters in the bureaucracy.

During his military service, he focused on local customs and daily life, even on his journey into exile. In "On My Way to Exile in the South" he wrote about a temple, dialects, water, stones, and houses in the area. In one episode he stays briefly at a temple, resting in a monk's cell, where incense burned. The smoke arouses in him desire for a cigarette, but when he takes a puff the monk looks uncomfortable. Yi argues that in a deep sense incense and cigarette smoke are no different. How can we know whether Sakyamuni likes only the smoke of incense, not cigarettes? Each form of smoke produces its own pleasure. The monk is persuaded in the end. This story may seem trivial, but Yi's belief that the sacred (incense) and mundane (cigarette) are equal is hardly trivial.

Yi's emphasis on the importance and originality of local customs goes beyond mere difference. During his military service in Samga district, he wrote in his spare time *Pongsŏng Munyŏ*, introducing local customs, diverse ways of life, eighty tools, and vivid descriptions of the cultural landscape of Yŏngnam Province. "Sketch of a Market" is often compared to "On My Way to Exile to the South." Unlike the daily market in Seoul, village markets in other parts of the Chosŏn dynasty opened every five or seven days, and all the townspeople gathered there on market days. Yi seems to have a special interest in crowded places, and since he stayed nearby he could observe people coming and going to the market. He sees "a man dragging a cow," "a man holding a bag of rice," and "a man carrying a bundle of herring." He catalogues dozens of people, as if determined not to miss a single one. This is no value judgment. His readers experience the local market and begin to grasp differences between local people and people in Seoul. Yi's appreciation of everyone and everything allowed him to bring to imaginative life the unique character of local people and the world around them.

After his forced military service, Yi wrapped up his life in Seoul and returned home, where the subjects of his writing changed to natural things, as if he had no lingering affection for humanity. His later writings are collected in *Paekunp'il* and *Yŏnkyŏng*, the latter being an encyclopedia of tobacco's origin, method of cultivation, tobacco goods and their use. "I am a tobacco-maniac," Yi wrote. Tobacco was at the time a hot item of personal preference regardless of sex. Yi seems to have grown tobacco in Namyang, which led him to write the only book about tobacco in the Chosŏn period.

Paekunp'il (A Short Sketch of Paekun) is a more free-style work, as the title indicates. If this way of writing was traditionally called p'ilgi and usually described people, no person appears in Yi's book. Nature, animals, and plants are the heroes of this book; various birds, fish, cattle, worms, flowers, grains, fruits, vegetables, trees and plants are described. Yi treats the vital force of these things with a deep sense of awe. To the insect living in the sorghum straw, he says, "Happy are you, insect! You are born here, eat here, dress here, and grow old here." He praises the insect's happy excursion, comparing his leisurely life in Namyang to that of the insect.

The Worlds of Yi Ok's Major Works

The World of *Kyŏnggŭm Sopu* (*Short Odes of Kyŏngkŭm*)

I have already mentioned that Yi wrote odes early in his career and how they differ from other writer's odes. Because pu writing was an examination subject, Yi must have written many odes during his days at Sŏnggyun'gwan. He left a great number of pu, reimagining the form by employing sop'ummun style.

His classmate, Kim Ryŏ, edited seventeen of these odes, noting that "Yi Ok's odes are far superior to those of other writers, who cannot compete with him." His odes deconstructed the traditional form, in their refusal to employ only rhymed verse and his decision to introduce a speaker in the beginning or the middle of a text. He even invented imaginary figures of people to converse with. Host and guest, imaginary character and personified animal and plant talk to each other, argue, and share their feelings. Yi successfully revealed the character of each thing, as well as his own ideas. Interlocution was a favorite literary technique in Korean literature in Classical Chinese. But this method had seldom been used in writing pu. Yi Ok's odes were thus unique.

Yi's structural variations of pu can be classified into three categories according to their contents: poems about animals and plants, poems about love and resentment between men and women, and poems about the history of the Korean peninsula. Because love and resentment between men and women is an important theme of Yi's works, I will elaborate on it below. "Samdobu" (Ode on Three Capitals), which treats the transfer of a past dynastic capital, is a rare example of Yi presenting his view of history. His most prominent odes concern animals and plants, which were important topics for him from his youth. But Yi displays a keener interest in them in his later writings, translating his feelings into them to capture their true character. For example, "An Ode Lamenting a Butterfly" commemorates a dead butterfly fluttering in the wind before drowning in a pond. The beautiful figure of the butterfly, the spring mood, the affectionate call "Butterfly, butterfly," the grief-ridden words—Yi's identification of the butterfly's death with falling petals demonstrates a level of dexterity few can imitate.

These odes are somewhat different from the works he wrote on animals and plants after his retiring to the country. Yi tended to interpret the reality of human society and its inner dynamics through the lenses of plants and animals. Thus he identifies insects chirping, the harbinger of fall, with a hapless poet's anger or the sorrow of a woman who misses her beloved. He compares a blood-sucking flea to a man who loses his mind for a small profit, and flies and mosquitoes caught in a spider's web to petty, crafty people or shameless officers who suck the life out of the lower class. These odes differ from his later ones in which he treats nature, plants, and animals without making any value judgment.

The World of *Plain Verses*

It is well known that women play a significant role in Yi Ok's writings, as subjects in his major works, the textures of which are tender and delicate, as if composed by a woman. The most important work, *Plain Verses*, has an unusual structure with three difficulties and four rhymes. Three difficulties explain why he wrote this work, and four rhymes sing the reality of women and their feelings.

When we read this work, the introductory "difficulties" catch our attention more than the main verses. Yi logically explicates the love between a man and a woman, as well as the woman's sincerity—the foundation of his creative work. In the first difficulty he argues that every man has his own name and work just as the ten thousand things of the universe have their own voices and colors. The second insists that nothing comes closer to human feelings in observing creation than the feelings between a man and a woman, the woman's being the sincerest. And the third difficulty argues that plain verse is the most useful in expressing women's feelings.

The first rhyme, "Graceful Rhymes," sings of an ordinary woman's marriage and domestic life, recognizing the universal desire for home. The second, "Beautiful Rhymes," expresses her desire to be beautiful through the application of make-up. "Libertine Rhymes" treat the lives of deviant women who break taboos. Yi thinks he cannot defend prostitutes in the red-light district; nothing can be done for those who engage in such behavior, and so he examines their joys and sorrows, and their situation. Finally, "Unspeakable Rhymes" depicts the wretched life of a woman married to a libertine whose behavior is beyond description. While speakers in the earlier section envy the opposite sex or express their longing, the libertine's wife is filled with resentment. She advises women not to marry a petty official, a soldier, a translator, or a merchant, because they are often away from home. But she envies them, because her husband is a rake who indulges himself in drinking and gambling. Unlike other men, this monster does not travel but stays at home to assault her psychologically and physically. Hopeless, she seeks a divorce, but her in-laws make it impossible for her to leave. The sorrow of this miserable woman seems to summarize the lives of woman in the Chosŏn period. Yi portrays a diverse range of human actions and feelings through the lens of a woman's psychology and her reality.

The Story of Student Sim and Other Stories

Yi Ok's stories invite us to imagine the broad scope of humanity. "The Story of Student Sim" is a short novel in the form of chŏn (a life story) depicting love between Sim and a nameless woman. Love stories of men and women were written before the Chosŏn period, usually portraying the love and longing of a handsome man and a beautiful woman. "The Story of Student Sim" belongs to the same genre as the so-called "accounts of love," and since it narrates love between a man and a woman, it is also a sort of extended version of *Plain Verses*.

The two protagonists miss each other until they come to a tragic end. It is noteworthy that the description of their meeting and love comprises two-thirds of a problematic story. They first meet at the intersection of Unjong Street and the Kwangt'ong Bridge, the most crowded site of floating populations in the late Chosŏn period. She is a daughter of a middle-class family living in Sojugong-dong, and Sim is the eccentric descendant of the nobility. Sensing his nightly presence, she tosses and turns in her bed, unable to sleep for almost a month. They communicate silently through the wall that separates them before they finally sleep together, knowing their love cannot work out because, as she says, she is "a mere daughter of a middle-class family." But their love inspires them to spurn any obstacle, dreaming of a love that transcends class difference.

If "The Story of Student Sim" concerns the star-crossed love and despair of a man and a woman, Yi's other stories portray in similar ways the fates of court and commoner women, gisaengs, scholars, advanced classicists, handicapped people, singers, Buddhist monks, and swindlers—ordinary people, that is. He focuses on the fate of those who cannot avoid what fortune has in store for them and their attempts to cope. If the uncontrollable fate of anyone finds best expression in his or her actions, Yi has limitless compassion for those who are doomed by their destiny.

Another characteristic of Yi's stories is his deep insight into human nature. He attributes the unswerving loyalty practiced by lower-class characters to their purity; discusses the entangled feelings between men and women; and disapproves of those who cheat others and go with the flow of a corrupt time. Yi does not highlight good and evil in human nature but emphasizes instead that people differ from one another according to their nature and temperament.

Lastly, Yi explores the difficulty of meaningful encounters. Certain that having relationships with others is inevitable as long as one is human, he studies these relationships in many stories. Some find redemption through harmonious meetings, some run into trouble through a wrong meeting, some change their fate in a meeting. Yi's works calmly illustrate that good meetings are rare and finding a true friend is scarcely possible. Human relationships are incomplete—and always floating.

Yi Ok's Place in the History of Korean Literature

Kim Ryŏ, who collected and published Yi Ok's works, notes that "Yi's peculiar feelings and novel thoughts emerge as a silkworm throws up thread and spring water bubbles up from a hole." He adds, "Yi's writing is delicate where emotions and thoughts spring up, and his poetry is clear and light with a sharply refined dignity." Praising another's writing is common, but Kim's criticism of Yi's work is appropriate. Yi's thought is original, his writing style is lively.

The following four traits summarize Yi Ok's place in classical Korean literature. First, he reached the summit of sop'ummun in the late Chosŏn period. He had a firm conviction about his identity as a sop'ummun writer, arguing that "If you study ancient prose, you will fall into falsity." He thought an old writing style could not portray a changing world, representing things as they really are. His sop'ummun was original in both style and content, because he wrote what he wanted to write.

Secondly, Yi charted new terrain in literature, exploring the true nature of the human condition through the naming of things. Others wrote about this, but none pursued it as whole-heartedly as Yi. He did not hesitate to use local dialects or market slang to reveal the true nature of experience, enlarging this way of proceeding to include things, animals, and plants. Thus he created a human-centered narrative by placing it within the grand harmony of the ten thousand things of the universe.

Thirdly, Yi devoted himself to the study of human nature and ecology with his own egalitarian perspective. He treats all his writing subjects equally whether they are men or women, lower- or higher-class people, or animals and plants. He approaches them not from his own perspective but from theirs. This is a very important point. Because most intellectuals and writers of the Chosŏn dynasty were from the ruling upper class, they regarded lower-class people as people to rule over or protect. The so-called aeminsi (poems praising commoners) derives from this attitude. Yi's contemporary Chŏng Yakyong, a scholar of practical learning, is famous for poems depicting the hardships of the common people, whom he regards from on high. Yi does not look down on any person, plant, or animal but approaches them from the same eye-level of each being.

Fourthly, Yi created the literature of common people in the late Chosŏn period. As a descendant from a concubine line, Yi could not work as a government official and was keenly aware of his lot as a marginalized intellectual. He did not reveal his opinions about current social issues or politics. Instead, he wrote mainly about the daily lives of common people and natural things. Nor he did make value judgments of good or evil about them. Instead, he sympathized deeply with them as the repetitive use of exclamatory phrases such as "I feel sad" or "It's regrettable" shows. A petit bourgeois himself, he represented faithfully the life of common people in his works.

Hwan-kuk Jung
Professor of Korean Language and Literature
Dongkuk University

Short Odes of Kyŏnggŭm

The Later Part of an Ode on a Frog's Croaking

The guest, blaming the host, said,
"Your 'Ode on a Frog'[1] is
both eloquent and subject to dispute.
It's a pity I couldn't let stupid Sima[2] hear it.
But this is also foolishness.
If we approach it from a normal point of view,
frogs croak on their own;
they feel nothing for either the public or the private realm.
When you try to make fun of their disagreeable sound,
you praise their foolishness instead.
I'd like to discuss this matter with you again.
"Do you know the hidden meaning of a frog's croaking?"

The host replied,
"It's knowable.
You hear noise
where people gather, don't you?"
They fill the marketplace in the market
and the capital, in the capital city.
If you hear them from a distance
the noise is like boiling soup.
But if you listen carefully, each
and every sound rises from their bowels:

---

[1] The title and dialogue of this poem suggest there was a first part to "Ode on a Frog's Croaking," which seems not to have been handed down.
[2] When Emperor Huidi of the Jin dynasty was in Hualin Garden, he heard frogs croaking, and asked if they cry for the public or in private. Palace attendant Guyin replied, "If they are in a public place, they cry for the public, and if they are in the private place, they cry in private." Sima was the family name of Jin royalty, which here refers to Emperor Huidi.

the sad sound of grieving,
the crazed sound of drunkenness,
the merry sound of singers,
the angry sound of argument.
The sound comes
from the very place where emotion resides.
Frogs are like people,
their sounds rising from inside.
If we look into their emotions from this point of view,
it is clear as daylight.
In "Six Canons" of *The Rites of the Zhou Dynasty*,
the ministry of punishment oversees punishment;
Keokssi[3] spread ash
and remove frogs and tadpoles.
Frogs croak perhaps because they are afraid of this.
When Kuch'ŏn,[4] King of Yue dynasty, led
his soldiers into the Wu country,
he encountered angry frogs,
and expressed courtesy to them on the crossbar of his wagon.
Frogs croak perhaps because they are moved by this.
When Chibaek[5] opened a waterway to Chinyang
to overthrew Cho Yangja, frogs lost their homes
and had to spawn on the stone steps
and yards of living people.[6]

---

[3] 蝦氏 Yushi was a public office in charge of removing frogs and narrow-mouthed toads. The name derives from the family names of the first official to take the position, Yu.

[4] Goujian (句踐) was the king of the Kingdom of Yue near the end of the Spring and Autumn period.

[5] 智伯 Zhibo : A high minister of the Jin dynasty, whose name was Yao. He was later defeated by Zhao Xiangzi (趙襄子), one of the high ministers of the Jin dynasty.

[6] Refers to Zhibo (智伯)'s flooding of the citadel in Jinyang. Frogs spawned in the flooded kitchens.

Frogs croak perhaps because they are heavy-hearted about this.
In the fifth year of Wŏnjŏng,[7]
when the general mounted a military expedition to the South,
frogs fought in the capital of the Han dynasty,
as the omen has shown.
Frogs croak perhaps because they are angered by this.
Zhuang Zi's frog mistook the inside of the well
for the northern sea
and boasted of his place
to a turtle in the eastern sea.[8]
If we consider this, then we may say
that frogs croak because they are arrogant.
Kong Tŏkchang's[9] frogs
became small drums and reed instruments,
like the pipe and drum music of Yangpu[10]
when the moon is white and a clean wind blows.[11]
If we consider this, then we may say
that frogs croak because they are merry.
Their noise is
similar to an angry shout, an infant's cry,

---

[7] 112 B.C. 元鼎 Yuanding is the era name of the Han dynasty Emperor Wudi. Frogs and toads fought that fall, and in the spring 100,000 soldiers campaigned in the Southern Yue, securing nine regions.

[8] The frog at the bottom of the well (井底之蛙) is a fable by Zhuang Zi 莊周, sometimes known as "looking at the sky down a well."

[9] Kong Dezhang (孔德璋) is Kong Zhigui (孔稚圭), a man of letters in the Southern Qi Dynasty. He enjoyed artistic elegance and let his garden grow wild.

[10] Refers to the court ritual music played in China, with musicians seated on stage or standing below.

[11] One day Kong Dezhang heard frogs croaking in the garden. When people asked him why he did not weed his garden, he said the croaking frogs were the music of Yangbu.

the call of geese, the call of ducks,
the sound of cross flutes, the sound of chaeng.[12]
The noise is louder when the wind is cooler than usual,
and rings our ears when the rainy season ends.
It may seem to have no reason,
but it has a reason of its own.
If you don't believe me,
empty your mind and listen to it."

The guest laughed and said,
"You know only one thing in your ignorance of other things.
What feelings do they possess to make the sounds of *agak* or
  kkwaekkkwaek?
Though they swell their bellies, taper their heads to a point,
carry silk patterns, wear red and green colors,
and put on many-colored clothes with water chestnut patterns,
and live in cool, clean deep water;
and though their croaking is like the shouting of a brave man,
or the fluent talk of an eloquent speaker,
or the murmuring of a scholar or a literary man,
or the strong, clear outspoken comment of an honest vassal;
and though this sound
seems to bring about a certain action,
what they do—if you consider the consequences—
is just dig mud and run about the hole.

How, then, can you say they have any feelings when they croak?

The host rewarded him with this:
"What I said was a joke. How can I know?"

---

[12] A traditional Korean musical instrument with thirteen strings.

Ode on Ch'ilsŏk[13]
–Written for fun in the amatory style

Paulownia leaves fall
and autumn is all over the world.
As autumn wind blows,
Mars also flows.
What night is tonight?
It's the seventh day of the seventh month.
Tonight is the merry night when Chingnyŏ
travels West to meet her beloved.
When crows and magpies fly
across the Milky Way,
sacred rain drizzles down,
washing the fragrant carriage.
As clouds disappear from the road
and the silky twilight is taken from the mantle,
every spirit is purified
and stately things are everywhere.

---

[13] Ch'ilsŏk is the seventh day of the seventh month on the lunar calendar. It is said the Altair Star (Kyŏnu) and Vega Star (Chingnyŏ) meet once in a year on the night of Ch'ilsŏk, on Ojak Bridge, where crows and magpies perch. A daughter of the Crystal Emperor of Heaven, Chingnyŏ, was a weaver, and Kyŏnu was a diligent shepherd. But once they married, they indulged in nuptial pleasures instead of working. The emperor, angered, ordered them to live apart, east and west of the Milky Way, meeting only once a year on the seventh night of the seventh month of the lunar calendar. Taking pity on them, the crows and magpies pitched Ojak Bridge over the Milky Way so that Kyŏnu and Chingnyŏ could meet. It is said that rain falls on the night of Ch'ilsŏk and the next morning, thanks to their tears of joy and sorrow; no healthy crows and magpies are seen because they flew up to the Milky Way to build the bridge. This rite was performed to ensure a plentiful harvest and skillful weaving.

From the fluttering depths of her celestial gown,[14]
Chingnyŏ puts on a star-like chignon.
Wearing peach-like makeup,
and dangling moon-like jade decorations,
she advances in the procession[15]
as if in grief—and delight.
Why is the carriage so slow?
My mind travels faster than it does.
The bright Milky Way shows up before I do,
and Kyŏnu has already arrived.
On seeing my dear husband,
all is sorrow.
I send my grievances with the bluebird,[16]
complaining endlessly about my sorrows and grudges.

"Since our last happy encounter, the year has turned
while you were in the West and I was in the East.
The winter night is long, the moon shines white,
the spring day is beautiful, and the flowers are red.
The mandarin ducks are happily bathing and mating
while a lonely crane cries for her mate.
If this is true even for trivial animals,
how can humans live without affection?
When I look in the mirror in the morning my rosy face is crumpled,
and at night blue tears fall before the candle.
I am knitting anxiety on the loom where once I wove silk.

---

[14] 霞帔 (Hap'i): Pretty cloth worn by fairies in the celestial world.
[15] 鳳蓋 (Ponggae): Equipment and decorations for the King or High Officer's progress, used here as a metaphor for Chingnyŏ's journey.
[16] 青鳥 Qingniao : The legendary three-legged bluebird and a bearer of good news. It is said that as a messenger of 西王母 Xiwangmu, the bird delivered a letter to the royal court of the Han dynasty.

Thus it is only natural that the sound of the shuttle is seldom heard.
My fragrant pillow swallows my red tears,
and my maid is surprised at the scene I make every morning.
My flowery cheeks are unrecognizably gaunt,
and in my expression you can read my long-held grudge.
Unable to bury my anxiety and die,
I still look forward to meeting you again.
My weak stomach is sensitive to sorrow and joy,
my happiness grows a hundred times bigger when I meet you.
Our time for pleasure is limited
even if the water clock has not run out.
That we cannot enjoy this for a long time
only adds to my disappointment.

Pulling a sad face at what Chingnyŏ said, Kyŏnu sends a gentle answer:

Buddhists obey the law of perfect consummation,
and poets write poems on separating.
Flowers bloom and fall,
the moon waxes and wanes.
Since ancient times, beautiful rosy-cheeked women
have known no limit to their sorrow.
Emperor Shun's carriage once went south,
but Mt. Kuŭi[17] is green for no reason.
On the Sosang River,[18] where even bamboo grieves,

---

[17] 九疑山 Jiuyi Shan: A mountain south of Xiangshui (湘水), in Hunansheng (湖南省), China, close to Cangwu (蒼梧), where King Sue died. He is said to be buried on the mountain's sunlit southern slope.

[18] 瀟湘江: The Xiaoxiangjiang River

tears blind Ahwang and Yŏyŏng.[19]
Ye lost his elixir[20]
and cultivated his mind for enlightenment at Yodae.[21]
Ran bird[22] cries, laurel weeps,
and Soa[23] grieves in autumn.
What, then, is the point of mentioning
Yŏnch'ŏ of Ch'ogang [24] or Miss Yu, the showgirl from Zhangtai?[25]
For a stone, there is a statue of a woman petrified from waiting for a flower, the resurrection lily.
They suggest the ties of love rarely last,
the root of affection is easily damaged.
You're not the only one, dear lady,
to whom heaven dispenses sorrow.
Twenty thousand coins for our crime

---

[19] 娥皇 Ehuang and 女英 Nuying, the daughters of Emperor Yao, both married Emperor Shun. When Emperor Shun died on Cangwu, they jumped into the Xiaoxiangjiang River. Their tears smeared the bamboo trees, which thenceforth grew a new species of bamboo tree with black marks.

[20] 羿 Yi was a famous archer in Chinese mythology. When he did not return from a hunting trip, Henge swallowed the elixir called Jindan (金丹) and fled to the Palace in the Moon. There were nine suns in the sky at the time, but Yi, who had just shot down eight suns, could not shoot the remaining one.

[21] 瑤臺 Yaotai: The place in which fairies live.

[22] 鸞 luan : An imaginary bird in Chinese legend.

[23] 素娥 Sue: Chang'e's (嫦娥) other name (another name of Henge). She stole the elixir of Xiwangmu for her husband Yi. But she ate the elixir secretly and fled to the moon to become the moon fairy.

[24] Lianqi 蓮妻 of Chijiang 楚江: Unknown

[25] 柳 Liu of 章臺 Zhangtai: 韓翃 Han Hong, a poet in the Tang dynasty had a gisaeng whose surname was Liu. They were separated by the An Lushan Rebellion, and she became a Buddhist nun. Zhangtai was a prosperous street in Chang'an (長安) in Tang China.

and three thousand years in exile.
The Milky Way is so long and wide
it is vaguely adjacent to heaven.
I was charged with a crime,
and you're miserable.
But the verdict of heaven is final,
and our sorrow is useless.
Let's drink the flowing twilight
and enjoy this night.

Let's call all the ladies-in-waiting
to bring glasses for the party.
Nine rounds of wine, and yet we aren't drunk;
three times the music stopped, and yet we aren't happy.
In the blink of an eye the crescent moon disappeared in the East,
and the Milky Way hangs on in the West.
The heavenly cock cries once,
and sorrow strikes the whole company.
The horseman urges us on again,
the carriages are ready to go.
Crying once more, we climb into our carriages,
promising to meet again next year.
Tears stifled a thousand times
suddenly burst like a spring.
When we sprinkle them on the wind,
rain fills the human world.

Ode on a Turtle with a Preface
–Written in April, 1782

From ancient times the filial son
entrusted the turtle with a prayer for his father's longevity,
because the sacred turtle is long-lived.
But this is an allegory, which has nothing to do with the turtle—
is it close to not following the law?
On the first day of April 1782,
people gathered in Nakchijŏng Pavilion
for my father's 60th birthday party.
There was a turtle
with red eyes and a green body
cutely loitering in the yard.
When it stopped at the handrail of the window,
an unusually auspicious aura caught people's attention.
Everyone said,
"This auspicious thing regards the crane in the green field[26] as a slave
and competes with the South Star.[27]
We think the sky from a distance
has bestowed a gift upon our old man."
Overwhelmed with joy,
I'd like to celebrate this by writing a song lyric
to record the role of heavenly will in this.
On the first day of April 1782,
Chungnija's[28] father has lived long enough to enjoy his sixtieth birthday,
and I am at once very happy and concerned.

---

[26] Another name for a crane; an old crane was a symbol of longevity, like the turtle.
[27] The star controlling one's span of life.
[28] One of Yi Ok's pennames.

Fluttering about in my many-colored clothes,[29] I woke early in
   the morning,
invited many elders, and strained liquor through a sieve.
Then I opened the bamboo-twig gate wide,
and spread clean cushions,
and prepared everyone's seat except for one on the left,
and waited for my beautiful guests.
From out of nowhere one guest suddenly
arrived earlier than the others.
He was crawling,
he looked just like a hŭibi.[30]
He climbed onto the guest steppingstone
and stood there casually.
He stretched his neck as if to look far into the distance
and bowed politely with his hands folded.
Chungnija hurried down from his seat and courteously lifted his
   sleeves.
"May I ask who you are?"
The guest answered,
"I'm a man of the sea,
my name is Wŏnsŏ,[31]
and my government post is togu.[32]
I received the auspicious vital force of Puksu[33]
and live in the clear water of Nammyŏng.[34]

---

[29] The custom of grown children to wear many-colored clothes and mimic children to please their elderly parents on their birthdays.
[30] A large turtle with dark yellow dots.
[31] A nickname for a turtle
[32] An assistant to the director of the local government, who inspects officials and delivers the king's messages.
[33] Refers to the Big Dipper.
[34] A great sea in the south, mentioned in *Chuangzi*.

Emperor Yu of Xia met me to receive the Luo Inscription,[35]
and Zhougong listened to my advice in choosing where to live.[36]
People earn treasure with one cha[37] of me[38]
and make me auspicious with five colors.
Some are astounded when they use me as a bed support,[39]
others display my exquisite beauty to decorate a handle.
Traces of my previous bright life
are faithfully recorded in old books.
Now I have finally met my master.
But why was our meeting delayed for so long?"
Chungnija asked,
"Aren't you the head of three thousand crustaceans? You live far
 away. Why did you come here?"
The guest replied,
"Rumor has it
you're hosting a party,
inviting guests with dishes made of vegetables from the back
 yard
and praying for longevity with liquor brewed from mountain
 flowers.
Your desire to fulfill a son's duty is boundless,
and I pray for your father's health and a long life.

---

[35] Emperor Yu controlled flooding with the sacred turtle shell's forty-five patterns in the Luo Stream.
[36] Zhougong burned a turtle shell to divine the location of the capital of Zhou.
[37] A traditional unit of length, one cha is about 30.3 cm.
[38] King Yuan of the Song dynasty used a sacred turtle for divination and made its hide a national treasure.
[39] A story in Sama Qian's *Records of the Great Historians*: An old man in the south put a turtle under his bed to support it. After twenty years, the man died. When people moved the bed, they found the turtle still alive.

I received star energy from the old man at the South Pole[40]
and borrowed a sacred peach from Sŏwangmo.[41]
This is a very important party.
Delighted to hear about it,
I have come here
wearing my tidiest black clothes."
Chungnija said,
"You didn't mind travelling a thousand li—why?"
The guest answered,
"Yes, I've heard that people always pray
for longevity at a birthday party.
Some prayed against the sacred ch'un tree,[42]
some drew cranes to symbolize longevity.
There is only one thing
worth offering in this place.
I have lived a long time, watched
and enjoyed longevity among the ten thousand things.
Like the sky and earth, I neither died,
nor grew old, nor turned pale as the sun and moon and stars.
I felt sorry for the early deaths of Kaeng[43] and Tam,[44]

---

[40] Refers to the South Star, which controls one's life span.
[41] 西王母 Xiwangmu: The Queen Mother of the West tends a sacred peach tree, which bears fruit once every three thousand years. If you eat this fruit, you will live forever.
[42] A type of tree that blooms white flowers in the summer and has edible leaves. In *Chuangzi* it is said to live eight thousand years in one spring and eight thousand years in one fall—a figure for a father and longevity.
[43] 鏗 Keng: A vassal to Emperor Yao, he was said to have lived eight hundred years.
[44] 聃 Dan: Laozi's name. He was said to come from his mother's womb after eighty years of pregnancy and enjoyed 150-250 years of life.

and regarded Prince Kyo[45] and Akchŏn[46] as children.
I planted heavenly peach seeds and ate their fruit,
tamed the crane's eggs and rode on their black wings.
Once I loitered by the Palhae Sea,[47]
mulberry fields turned green nine times in the eastern sky,
and I came back to rest on the lotus flowers.
Dawn broke white and twilight reddened many times.
I met the Great Jade Emperor at Chado[48]
and mentioned my age in a discussion about my health.
I searched for ch'un trees and, when the flowers fell,
piled up counting sticks to block the sky.
No one who lives in this world
has enjoyed longevity like me.
I ask you to allow me
to offer my longevity to your father."

Chungnija was happy—and deeply moved.
He poured liquor for his guest and sang a song of gratitude.
"I have a beautiful guest ["Nongmyŏng"[49]],
who is already drunk ["Kich'wi[50]"],

---

[45] 喬 Qiao: The crown prince of King Ling of the Zhou dynasty, known as an immortal hermit. He enjoyed playing a reed instrument that made the sound of a crane's cry. He disappeared into the cloud riding on the wings of a crane.
[46] 偓佺 Woquan: A Taoist hermit in the ear of Emperor Yao.
[47] 渤海 the Bohai Sea: The innermost gulf of the Yellow Sea and Korea Bay on the coast of northeastern and north China.
[48] 紫都 Zidu: The capital of the Great Jade Kingdom.
[49] 鹿鳴: The title of a poem in "Minor Court Hymns, 小雅" in *The Book of Songs*.
[50] 既醉: The title of a poem in "Major Court Hymns, 大雅" in *The Book of Songs*.

and offers us the great blessing ["Ch'oja"[51]]
of longevity["Yŏlcho"[52]].
My father and mother ["Ilwŏl"[53]]
will surely live until they are quite old["Namsanyudae"[54]]."

The guest washed his cup out to pour more liquor and answered with a song:
"It's summer in April ["Sawŏl"[55]],
and I climbed a government building ["Ch'ilwŏl"[56]]
to pray for longevity ["Ch'ilwŏl"].
Boundless blessings fall ["Yŏlcho"],
which will live for a thousand years and then another thousand ["Pigung"[57]]
on the mountain ridge and hill ["Ch'ŏnbo"[58]].

When he finished his song, he bowed twice and moved back, saying
"'I have bestowed longevity on you. It's time for me to leave."

---

[51] 楚茨: The title of a poem in "Minor Court Hymns, 小雅" in *The Book of Songs*.

[52] 烈祖: The title of a poem in "The Sacrificial Odes of Shang, 商頌" in *The Book of Songs*.

[53] 日月: The title of a poem in "The Odes of Pei, 邶風" in *The Book of Songs*.

[54] 南山有臺, 日月: The title of a poem in "Minor Court Hymns, 小雅" in *The Book of Songs*.

[55] 四月: The title of a poem in "Minor Court Hymns, 小雅" in *The Book of Songs*.

[56] 七月: The title of a poem in "The Odes of Pin, 豳風" in *The Book of Songs*.

[57] 閟宮: The title of a poem in "The Odes of Lao, 魯頌" in *The Book of Songs*.

[58] 天保: The title of a poem in "Minor Court Hymns, 小雅" in *The Book of Songs*.

Ode on the Sound of an Insect
—Written after Ku Yangsu's "Ode on an Autumnal Sound"[59]

While Mr. Yi[60] was sitting silently at midnight,
in the chill of autumn,
with every sound in the universe hushed,
suddenly there came a sound
from the four walls.
At first, it was like a whispering
and then it grew into a plaintive chirping.
It was like the subdued cry of a woman
who lost her husband or who was deserted by her husband.
It was like the restrained cry of wandering spirits
and dead souls, full of agony and resentment.
It was like a government official who was slandered and lost his job
or a miserable poet bitterly reciting lines, unable
to sleep in his longing for home.

Mr. Yi sighed at the sound and said,
"This is the chirping of insects.
Did you enter the hall in October
to let us know the end of the year is at hand?[61]
Do you cry ch'okchik[62] in advance against the coming cold
in your concern for humankind?
Is it like a faithful vassal's anxiety over the state of affairs

---

[59] 歐陽修: Ouyang Xiu, a Northern Song period writer and politician. "Ode to an Autumnal Sound" (秋聲賦) sings of the demise of all things in the chill autumn wind.
[60] Refers to the author himself.
[61] A citation from "July" in "The Odes of Pin, 豳風" in *The Book of Odes*: "In October, crickets enter under the floor."
[62] Onomatopoeia of a cricket's chirping. Literally, (促織) "to weave quickly," because it is cold; also a nickname for a cricket.

that you wait for autumn and chirp?
Is it to help relieve the sorrow of a scholar in autumn
that you move people with a plaintive sound?
Because you live a clean life, hidden from the world,
you leave a cool, clear trace.
Because you live on grass, not a salary,
your mind is empty, mysterious.
It's not at all unnatural that I grieve
over your chirping.
Though you're but a little creature,
you were born of heaven, too.
Though the sound comes from you,
heaven is, in reality, weeping through your body.
It's not your own sound
but heaven's affection.
Why does heaven allow you to cry
and make me feel this way?
Are you embarrassed that the great doctrine has not spread
because wind and rain ignore commands?
Do you condemn the world's frivolous customs and feel sad
that its end is at hand and people don't obey the laws of nature?
Do you console wanderers who beg for food
because you feel sorry about this year's meager harvest?
Do you lament the gradually strengthening yin
and mourn the looming demise of yang?
Or do you chirp because people don't know their anxiety
piles up like a mountain or a castle
to fill heaven's heart and stir its bowels?
How petty of you to borrow the tongues of insects
to plaintively ring in their bowels!
You make an upright scholar grieve in autumn
and a woman missing her lover cry at midnight at your chirping.
Ah, how you are alone among the ten thousand things
crying on behalf of heaven?

Orioles cry in spring
to make us pure and simple.
Cicadas cry in summer
to relax us and help us forget our pain.
Even little creatures like earthworms at dawn
and frogs in the evening don't make us feel sad.
But why do you alone cry in autumn
and overwhelm us with worry?
Is it because prosperity and decline
are caused by changes of time and luck
and even heaven cannot do anything about it?
Why don't you stop your chirping
and tell me about it in detail?
I've asked you a couple of times,
but you remain silent as a deaf mute.
I'd like to ask heaven about it,
but what can it say to me?
The desolate sound of autumn rain rings,
making the sound of insects louder.

Ode on Cursing Malaria

By chance, I came down with malaria in 1783. For three months I tried every possible remedy, unable to find a cure. Lying face down on a pillow, uttering nonsense in my delirium, I wrote a poem cursing malaria. But what I wrote is trifling, closer to a curse, inferior to Kwanjung's crab.[63] Punishing a disease with a pen, besieging it with Chinese ink—this is exhilarating, even if only for a little while. One way or another, it can make you forget your palsy.

Oh, the King of Kings loves his people
and always cares for them when they fall sick.
Though my body is small and feeble,
heaven takes care of it.
When I came down on a silver baby dragon,
I drove the horse after the Red Emperor.[64]
My parents raised me with grace,
lovingly wrapping me in swaddling clothes,
and when I grew up and put on regular clothes,
they warned me against drunkenness and socializing with thieves.
Thanks to them, I was saved from stubborn foolishness
as my bones and muscles grew stronger.
Stricken several times by the calamity of hopelessness,
I quickly recovered without medication.
But why do I lie in my bed and moan all May this year?

---

[63] 關中 Guanzhong: A historical region in China corresponding to the lower valley of the Wei River. There were no crabs in this region, though one house had a dried crab, which everyone feared. Malarial patients would borrow it to hang above the door and then be cured.
[64] Red Deity (赤帝), a cosmological *Wufang Shangdi* (五方上帝) god of Chinese religion.

Blame an unworthy descendant of King Koyang,[65]
dark and foolish and wicked Hŏmo[66]
who controls malaria in this world.
Those who have the bad luck to meet him
oscillate between hot and cold flashes.
A little while ago, a cart left from the snow country
and its flag stopped in Yŏmsan[67] at dawn.
At first it struck my shoulders lightly
and made a row at yiwhan.[68]
As southern middlemen go to market,
so it counts the days between intervals.
Nothing is more critical to self-healing than poetry;
hence Tu Po lay down, crying in pain.[69]
Samjŏl[70] lost his exquisite marbles and a leather sack
while sleep talking in his jade-green carriage.[71]

---

[65] The penname of King Zhuanxu (顓頊), one of the mythical Five Emperors 五帝. Here the unworthy descendant of King Koyang refers to the god of malaria.

[66] 虛耗, empty, wasting. Here Yi personifies malaria.

[67] 燄山 Yanshan, a legendary volcano. See 郭璞 Guopo's 山海經 *Shan Hai Jing*, a collection of myths, geography, animals, plants, minerals, witchcrafts, religion, history, and folklore.

[68] 泥丸 Niwan, the place where the god of the mind dwells in Taoism.

[69] 杜甫, Tu Fu. At the age of forty he suffered a severe bout of malaria: "Irksome malaria for more than three years, / The god of this disease knows no death, / My flesh and bones ache every other day, / and chill invades me as if I am embracing snow and frost." There is a story in 葛立方, Ge Li Fang's 韻語陽秋古今詩話, that Tu Fu, meeting a man suffering from malaria, told him that if he recited his poem he would be cured. The man recited "Tan Chajang's bones and skeleton were covered with blood. / I scattered them and returned to High Minister Choe," and he was healed.

[70] Literally, someone with three outstanding skills, though it is uncertain to whom this refers.

[71] The allusion to this anecdote is unknown.

When I removed my disease and examined its roots
I found that old books said the same thing.
The doctor who examined me
said it must be malaria.
A reckless ghost invaded a scholar
and made him sick:
it doesn't care if needles are inserted like a hedgehog,
it regards strong medicine like a soft drink.
An amulet painter curses it,
black ink like blood fills the paper.
Kitchen maids treat it tenderly,
daily offering it spoonfuls of chicken.
Citizens pray loudly to expel it,
employing every means at their disposal—
in vain—and so it has come to this.
Unable to bear the pain,
I would appeal to the Great Jade Emperor.
Now the wind is a horse quick as a thunderbolt,
and my mind, entrusted to a butterfly, is easy and elated.
Hongyong[72] consoles me in my seediness,
and I brush aside Ch'ŏng'ye[73] to knock on the jade door.
Fluttering about in my brilliant clean black clothes,
I run to the Chajŏng,[74] bowing down before the elders.
"I am your people, I committed small sins,
and heaven spared me calamities.
But I have lately met misfortune—a monster
corrupting my blood and spirit, leaving me a hunchback.
Please take pity on me,
send your spirit to clear it away,
not only for my comfort

---

[72] The animal that keeps the gate of heaven.
[73] A lion that keeps the jade door of heaven.
[74] The Great Jade Emperor's Palace.

but for the peace of the whole world."
The infuriated emperor betrays no anger,
showing instead his majesty by throwing his right sleeve.
He orders P'ungnyung[75] to beat the drum
and asks Ch'oyo[76] to ring the gong,
and at these sounds Chinmu[77] and Ch'ŏn'gang[78]
rush together.
Clouds gather, thunder strikes,
flags painted with clouds shine brilliantly,
pierced by bright starlight.
With Ch'am on the right and Ku on the left,[79]
he orders Ullu[80] to take hold of the sword.
Nat'a[81] boasts of his bravery, standing in front,
while Hyŏnnyŏ[82] defends the nine palaces from behind.
The noisy ghost soldiers number eighty thousand,
the deity generals, three thousand.
The wind blows solemnly,
descending with a fury.
That panic-stricken ghost
is not a tuna in the sea nor a sparrow hawk in the sky.
At the sound of a drum in heaven
nothing of the ghost is left for Ch'ulyŏn[83] to deal with.
His flowing blood forms red agate,
fluttering like maple leaves in the field.
After burying his flesh and bones in a cold dark prison,

---

[75] The god of thunder.
[76] The seven stars of the Big Dipper.
[77] Dark tortoise, god of the north.
[78] The god of thirty-six stars in the Great Bear in Taoism.
[79] Both are names of ghosts.
[80] The god of doors in an old Chinese legend.
[81] The god of law in Buddhism.
[82] A fairy who gave the emperor the tactics to fight Chiyou.
[83] The name of a precious sword.

they break and ground them up to burn.
They beat and behead those who committed cruelties
helping Kŏhŏ[84] and Somae.[85]
When they return to the Jade Palace with colors flying,
the happy emperor commends them.
When I bow and step back,
he says, "You, come forward.
You fell ill for no reason.
I pity you."
He gives me a greenish golden pill,
shining brightly with five colors.
I bow to receive it, return, and take the pill,
which will let me live for a hundred years free of illness.

---

[84] A ghost that causes epidemics.
[85] A one-footed goblin wandering at night.

Ode on a Fish
—Written in the summer of 1786

If the water world is a country,
then the dragon is the king.
Big fish like whales, kon,[86] and haech'u[87]
are vassals of the king.
Smaller fishes like catfish, carp, and pout
are petty officials and local clerks.
Those smaller than one cha[88]
are the citizens of this water nation.
It's no different than in the human world,
for there is also order between high and low
and the domination of big over small.
Thus when the dragon rules the country,
he never forgets to give rain when wells run dry during a drought.
To prevent overfishing and the elimination of some species,
he raises tall waves to cover them.
Hence nothing is not a form of grace
for fish.
Only one dragon is benevolent to fish,
while many large fish treat them ruthlessly.
Whales float with the tide, inhaling
small fish like poems and books.[89]
Monstrous snakes and crocodiles rush into the waves
to gulp and chew small fish, like produce from a farm.
Yellowfin gobies, mandarin fish, albino swamp eels, snakeheads—
all watch for their chance to sweep up
small fish, taking them like gold and silver.

---

[86] 鯤, a large legendary fish in Zhuangzi.
[87] 海鰌, a large legendary fish that controls the tide.
[88] A traditional unit of measure, one cha is about 30.3 cm.
[89] A metaphor for spiritual provisions.

The strong swallow the weak,
the high-born catch the low.
Unless they truly loathe such deeds,
no fish will survive.
Alas, without small fish
how can the dragon practice the role of the king,
And how can big fish show off?
Is this how the dragon
wards off species that kill them
instead of bestowing favors on them?
Ah, some think big fish exist only in water country,
not knowing they also exist in the human world.
How can you say a fish feeling sorry for humankind
is not the same as someone feeling sorry for them?

Ode on White Garden Balsam
–Written in the summer of 1786

That flower on the hill,
which is called "garden balsam,"
shiny as silk, carmine as cinnabar,
flutters lightly in its beauty.
When people pick it to dye their nails,
it's as if they have applied rouge.
It barely opens in the morning under the steppingstone
and always finds its place of an evening, before the mirror.
Ah, women's hands are like frost,
picking leaves and stems, leaving nothing unspoiled.
Only one blossom
stands apart.
It looks like snow that doesn't melt,
like jade that isn't soiled.
Brother of the cold Japanese apricot flower,
it's an esteemed friend of the lovely pear blossom.
It leaves a thin slanting shadow in moonlight
and a clean fragrance after rain.
Because it's white,
it's no good for dyeing fingernails red.
Women regard it
like ordinary grass.
Lightly they twirl their skirts, refusing to pick the flower
since it withers on the bush.
It meets butterflies, enjoys itself,
and may grow old in the gentle wind.
Ah, all your kin are red or purple—
why are you white?
All your kin are cut or snapped off—
why are you spared?
Do you refuse the bustling

and rambling, exalting above the world,
because the silky peach blossoms wither early on
and frost-bitten chrysanthemums later fade?
Do you hide your virtues and play down your beauty
to preserve yourself, discretely,
because trees are ravaged in blue and yellow[90]
and orchids burned for their fragrance?
Ailanthus and dentata oak are no good for timber,
because they grow crookedly.
Isn't their uselessness
what saves them?
As the four old men of Sangsan ate grass and mushrooms to slight the Han dynasty[91]
and Paegi ate bracken to soil the Zhou dynasty,[92]
so they have nothing to seek in this world,
because they have transcended it?
Ah, I look into you and find
you have many uses.
People grind you into powder
with which to draw a picture on a skirt,
and ferment you into liquor
fine enough for a libation on the sacrificial table.

---

[90] "A hundred-year-old tree is felled to make wine glasses, then painted blue and yellow, with the remaining stumps tossed into the ditch." *Zhuangzi*.

[91] The four men retired to Sangsan (商山, Shangshan) at the end of the Qin dynasty. When the first king of the Han dynasty (漢高祖) asked them to come out, they did not respond, and continued living on grass and mushrooms.

[92] 伯夷 Bo Yi: A retired scholar in the Yin dynasty, who tried to dissuade King Wu of Zhou from launching an attack. Ashamed of eating the food of the Zhou dynasty, he retired to Suyang Mountain 首陽山 (Shouyangshan) with his brother Shuqi and ate bracken only to die of hunger.

If they have your oil,
they can put it into meat soup.
If they harvest your root,
it can heal sores.
Your every blossom and leaf
are good and important,
and you have no reason to be disappointed
even when girls don't appreciate you.
Maybe it's heaven's will
to let you linger for a while as a light,
feeling sorry for the fading colors of spring.
Boys, keep this flower safe and whole.
I've written this up in detail for the impurity of this dusty world.

Ode on Ch'oryong[93]

A dragon is mysterious, difficult to understand.

Sometimes it becomes a drum,
sometimes a cane,
sometimes a swift horse,
and sometimes a sword blade.
It frequently changes shape,
and these changes never end.[94]
As for plants:
the eye becomes a rare fruit,[95]
the brain an exquisite fragrance,[96]
a tree spreads spots like scales,[97]
and grass unfurls its long beard.[98]
If you get just one of these,
you can boast of its fragrance.
The vigor of grape vines wriggling forth
is exceptionally lovely.
But they cannot be compared to you,

---

[93] 草龍, grass dragon, which refers to a grape.
[94] In myth and legend, the word "dragon" was used as an adjective for the most powerful and exquisite things: for example, dragon drum, dragon cane, dragon horse, dragon sword.
[95] Seems to refer to longan, which is called 龍眼, dragon eye.
[96] Seems to refer to the dipterocarp, which is called 龍腦香, dragon brain scent.
[97] Old pine bark that resembles the scales of a dragon. An old pine tree is called 龍鱗, dragon scale.
[98] When the emperor became an immortal hermit and ascended to the sky riding a dragon, his vassals held the dragon's beard to ascend. The beard that fell to the ground was said to become sago pondweed (*stuckenia pectinate*), which is called 龍鬚草, dragon beard grass.

not a dragon, but with a dragon in your name.
Your old vine first spreads
then scatters twigs in disarray;
exactly like a long tail,
it wraps around clouds and draws fog.
When leaves bud in April
and pile up,
you shine brilliantly
as fine fish scales.
Your furious beards[99] point to the sky,
entangling and tugging one other.
You resemble the beautifully colored sideburns of a dragon,
which people clutch as they ascend Chŏngho.[100]
Your grown fruits shine like stars,
they are so transparent we can see their marrow,
each a bright moon bead
like the cintamani in a dragon's jaw.[101]
When the clear wind shakes them,
their twigs and leaves flung inside out,
they rise and fall dizzily
as if they are fighting at the Chŏngmun.[102]
When the crescent moon shines,
casting their shadows on the empty yard,
kyuryŏng shakes its head,

---

[99] Refers to the tendrils of a grape.
[100] 鼎湖 Dinghu: According to legend, the place where the Yellow Emperor Huangdi Sheng ascended into the sky riding a dragon.
[101] Here Yi is comparing the shape of the grape to the cintamani of a dragon.
[102] Here Yi describes the shape of the clusters of grapes through an old story borrowed from the Zheng dynasty. But the details are unknown.

as in the painting of Lord Sŏp.[103]
When the morning dew forms beads,
adding green to the leaves,
they slide down
like rain.
When evening draws smoke
to press the racks and fill the ladder,
it reflects dim light
as if to ascend into the sky.
When I study your shape,
your figure,
grape, grape!,
you are indeed
a dragon among plants.

Ah, can this be a dragon?

A dragon becomes a dragon
not by its shape but by its virtues.
If you chase after the figure,
not its virtues,
even a flower can become a phoenix
and a tree, a giraffe.
If you can find four sacred animals[104] in the forest,
how can they be sacred and auspicious?
Alas, the world has fallen for appearances for so long—
who can discern the truth now!

---

[103] Qiulong 虬龍 is a baby dragon with horns on both sides, shining red. Lord Sŏp loved dragons and drew or carved dragons and dragon patterns in his house.
[104] The four sacred animals in the legend are the giraffe, phoenix, turtle, and dragon.

Ode on a Spider

In the cool of the evening Mr. Yi took a walk in his yard and
 found a spider.

With gossamer floating under the eaves,
the spider spun a web from the stalk of a sunflower,
weaving vertically and horizontally
the guiding rope and strings,
more than a cha wide,
its system up to grade.
It was neither dense nor light,
but dexterous and bizarre.
Mr. Yi thought the machine mind had built it
and raised his stick to tear it apart.

When he was about to throw it away, he heard it cry:

"I weave my thread
to fill my stomach.
What makes you
want to harm me?"

Mr. Yi, angered, said,

"Because you set a trap to kill living beings,
you're the enemy of insects.
In removing you,
I can do something good for them."

Then it laughed and spoke again.

"Ah, is it because the fisherman is wicked
that fish in the sea are caught

in the net he sets?
How can U'in's[105] order be wrong—
that wild animals caught
in a trap he set be placed on the butcher's table?
How can the judge be wrong
for sentencing people to prison
when he enforces the law?
Why don't you quarrel over Pokhwissi's[106] net,
or deny Paegik's burning,[107]
or blame Koyo for establishing the penal system?"[108]

What difference is there between me and them? Do you know
 what kind of creatures are in my net?

Butterflies are truly prodigal figures;
they wear makeup to deceive the world.
They love flourishes, flattering
white flowers, playing the coquette to red flowers.

Which is why I catch them in my net.

Flies are petty.
Jade is also slandered by them.

---

[105] A petty official in charge of forests, gardens, and games.
[106] 伏羲 Fuxi, one of the Three Sovereigns in Chinese mythology, is said to have created humanity and invented hunting, fishing, and cooking. He taught the ancient Chinese how to domesticate animals.
[107] 伯益 Boyi: A hero of Chinese mythology. As an U'in, he hunted animals and helped control flooding. When Emperor Shun tried to appoint him as his successor, he fled to the mountain. Mencius wrote: "Shun appointed Boyi as the official in charge of fire. When he burned a mountain cottage, animals escaped."
[108] 皋陶 Gao Yao, Minister of Law for Emperor Shun, established the penal and prison systems.

They lose their lives in wine and meat,
they never tire of loving profits.

Which is why I catch them in my net.

Cicadas are pure and honest,
like scholars.
But they never stop singing loudly,
showing off their voices.

Which is why I catch them in my net.

Bees are like wolves and wild dogs;
with honey and swords in their bodies,
absurdly they go in and out of government offices,[109]
always coveting spring flowers in vain.

Which is why I catch them in my net.

Mosquitos are the sneakiest,
like Toch'ŏl;[110]
hiding by day, emerging at night
to suck people's sweat and blood.

Which is why I catch them in my net.

Dragonflies have no manners;
like a frivolous young nobleman,
they have no time to sit calmly,
but fly off suddenly like a whirlwind.

---

[109] This phrase compares bees flying in and out of a hive in the morning and evening to officials entering and leaving a government building.

[110] An imaginary beast that devours human beings.

Which is why I catch them in my net.

Also the tiger moth's love of disaster,
the drosophila's love of work,
the firefly's empty boast about its light,
the longihorn beetle's sly theft of its name,[111]
the crowd of mayflies wearing bright clothes,
and the scarabs' blocking cartwheels—
they all cause catastrophes,
they don't know how to avoid it.
Their bodies are caught in the net,
their liver and brains paint the ground.
Ah, since this is not the time of Sŏnggang,[112]
we must use our penal system.
Because humans are not hermits or Buddhas,
they cannot eat only vegetables.
It's their fault
to be caught in a net.
How can you hate me
for setting a net?
Why do you love them
and reserve your anger for me?
Why do you interrupt me
and defend them?
Ah, you can't catch a giraffe
or lure a phoenix;
virtuous men should know the Way,
avoid crime and imprisonment.

---

[111] Longihorn's Korean name is Hanŭlso (Heavenly Cow). The line suggests that an insignificant insect like a longihorn stole "heaven" for its name.

[112] Refers to King Cheng (成王) and King Kang (康王) of the Zhou dynasty. During their reign, the world was peaceful, people committed no crimes, and punishment was not meted out.

Take heed!
Be prudent! Work hard!
Don't sell your name,
don't boast about your skills,
don't be greedy
or devote your life to gathering riches.
Don't be frivolous or foolish,
don't blame or envy others,
walk carefully,
come and go at appropriate times.
Otherwise there will be a bigger spider,
with a net a thousand, ten thousand times, larger than mine.

Upon hearing this,
Mr. Yi threw down his stick and ran away,
falling three times before he arrived at the threshold.
Only after he had locked the door
did he bend down and sigh.
The spider spins his thread
and continues as before, building another net.

Ode on a Dragon

An autumn day when the sea and sky are clear, and the air is jasper.
Is it to block traffic so that the dragon can appear to play?
Suddenly white rain dizzily sprinkles beads.
Is this because the dragon kicks the water to scatter it?
A dark cloud emerges from the ground and stands like a column.
Does the dragon leave the sea for the first time to ascend into the sky?
The west wind rises, it is three thousand chang[113] long.
Has the ascending dragon finally revealed this mysterious phenomenon?
The whole picture is unclear.
I concentrate, focusing on that direction.
The dragon's mane, scales, and spurting horns shine,
hang in the air, glow brilliantly.
It's dense up and down,
because the dragon's vassals guard it.
Because the dragon's ladies-in-waiting are summoned to the six-wheeled cart,[114]
they come in haste, creating a commotion.
All the deities monitor the dragon's progress,
many mountains loftily respond.
But these are the shapes of clouds,
imaginings of the people.
I wonder where they heard about it,
how these strange stories spread.
Only its long tail is connected,
it looks like a thousand-cha ch'oryŏn[115]

---

[113] One chang equals ten cha, about three meters.
[114] A six-wheeled cart that carries official documents and goods to the post office.
[115] White silk produced in the Chu dynasty.

hanging outside the cloud, clearly visible,
taking up the rear.
It's up and clotted, shaking lightly as if to show off,
hanging down, wriggling like a sluggish idler.
It circles slowly as if in longing,
winds around, suddenly pulls in the net.
Now it looks like a bow, now like an arrow,
now like a cord stretched out in the blink of an eye.
Clouds and fog scatter,
the thunder stills, the lightning ends.
The blue sea rolls on without cause,
and the red sun appears again.
It's lonely, empty, cool autumn weather;
they couldn't see the dragon's ascent, even if they wanted to.
How, then, can I follow it?
It rankles my heart, pierces my eyes.
Great is the dragon's virtue!
It soars leisurely up and down, bends down and circles.
If they can't see the dragon rise,
they'll say it's just a bit of floating cloud.
If the dragon doesn't hide but shows itself,
it will be no different than the mudfish and albino swamp eel
    swarming in the mud.
Sometimes the dragon moves, sometimes it's calm,
sometimes it appears, sometimes it shows itself.
Its shining, mysterious changes allow creation to prosper;
it creates public benefits and the whole world rejoices.
This is why people look up to the dragon
and regard it as sacred.
Who will be dragons among the people? Maybe a few talented
    men from ancient times—

Cha'ŭigaek[116] from the Tang dynasty, Kŭmmunyŏn[117] from the Han dynasty.
I can't find any others
facing a thousand-year-old darkness in the deepest cloud-energy.
Many had lofty horns and scales,
but they were just the makings of side dishes in Konggap.[118]
Ah, those poor men of the secular world!
How can they be worth discussing in the first chapter of *I Ching*?

---

[116] Seems to refer to Emperor Taizong 唐太宗 when he was the crown prince.

[117] Kŭmmun refers to Kŭmmamun (金馬門, golden horse gate) at the Weiyang Palace (未央宮) in the Han dynasty. Scholars waited there for royal commands.

[118] 孔甲 Kong Jia, the fourteenth king of the Xia dynasty. Because he liked ghosts and lewd things, feudal lords revolted against him. When a male and a female dragon came down from the sky, Yuryu (Liulei 劉累) learned from Hwanryongsi (豢龍氏 Huanlongshi) how to tame them and was awarded the surname Ŏryong (Yulong 御龍). He fermented the dead female dragon and offered it to the king.

Ode on a Flea

When Kyŏnggŭmja[119] rested after sunset
and felt at home in the dark,
moonlight shone brightly through the paper-sun window
and cool wind smeared the cotton blanket.
The buzzing sound of flies was no longer heard,
they were calm and complacent, like Zhuangzi's butterfly.
Feeling at ease, relaxing,
I went back and forth to Hwasŏ.[120]
Suddenly something
came through a gap in the cattail cushion,
moving noisily on the bamboo mat and blanket.
When I listened carefully,
the sound was like loud millet grains falling.
A little later, it clung to the ends of my hair and climbed,
valiantly, between my limbs and torso,
and stopped to crouch on my left shoulder,
quickly digging into my skin,
as if sewing seams with a silver needle.
As if I stumbled into a rosebush,
red thorns stung my skin,
my nerves and blood shrank in shock,
I couldn't bear it any longer.
I raised my hand to strike it,
scrubbed it into my armpit,
rubbed it,
and finally caught it with my thumb.
It wriggled under my fingernail,
determined to live.

---

[119] Another penname of Yi Ok.
[120] A utopia where the Yellow Emperor lingered in dream. People lived naturally, without a king or greed. He found enlightenment upon awakening, and thereafter ruled his country well.

I pitied it for not knowing calamity was near at hand. I struck its
   back in rebuke,

"Little creature,
you live in swarms in my bed and mat.
I haven't cleaned my house for three months,
because I'm lazy;
if you're thirsty, you can drink sweat,
if you're hungry, you can chew dead skin.
As a human being,
I was hardly lavish with you.
Why were you dissatisfied,
why did you attack me?
My blood isn't liquor—
how can I bear you pouring it out?
My skin is clean—
why do you poke me with your needle?
I don't understand you.
You can suck people's sweat and blood,
you know how to press our pressure points.
You live in dirt, buried in a crack,
move at night, stay hidden during the day.
You move forward on the wings of the situation,
with the machine mind of a hungry mouse.
You're wise as autumn mosquitoes
pursuing your profits.
You don't pass even a single thread,
and enter through the gap of a single stitch.
When you put your mouth to it,
your antennae don't miss the gap.

Even if P'yŏnjak[121] and Yubu[122] healed people
in the olden days with their needles,
they couldn't do it more adroitly than you.
You only know that people have flesh and blood,
but don't know the ferocity of their fingers and nails.
As ants build a hill, horseflies gather,
bees sting, and frogs crowd together,
you suck people's sweat and blood
to fill your stomach.
He who has eaten to the full collapses,
and he who hurries falls.
People let blood come from the marrow
of those who make their flesh bleed.
Filling your mouth and stomach
will lead to your downfall.
When I judge you separately from your deeds,
I wonder how you can be so wise.
But when I judge you from your later behavior,
I wonder how you can be so stupid.
Do you know how to love your mouth
but not your body?
Did you lose sight of the most important truth
in your trivial pursuit of profits?
You're not ignorant,
but your lust for material things has darkened you, no?
I'll open your stomach later
to look into your heart."
When I squashed it with my fingernail,
I heard something jump.
I urged my young body to get up and light the lamp.
When I looked at it,

---

[121] 扁鵲 Bian Que, a legendary doctor in the Han dynasty.
[122] 兪跗 Yu Fu, a famous doctor during the reign of the Yellow Emperor.

I couldn't find its stomach,
only blood resembling a peach blossom.

Second Ode on a Flea

After Kyŏnggŭmja caught the flea,
my dreams grew comforting.
I arranged the edge of my bedding,
tossing and turning in my hut.
An ascetic whose body was as big as a millet grain
leaped out like a flying bullet.
He had pointed cheeks
and a round belly,
and he wore burning red clothes.
He approached me and began to talk
sorrowfully,
"How is your dream?"
"Comforting."

The ascetic said,
"Ah, that's dangerous!
To be awake is to be alive,
to dream is to be dead.
If yin flourishes, the heavenly way sickens.
If the corporeal spirit[123] flourishes, human things sicken.
The admonition of deadwood and a wall of dung[124]
came from Confucius.
The proverb 'rising early in the morning and sleeping late at night'

---

[123] A spirit (魄) existing independently from the body belonging to yin. What belongs to yang is called the ethereal soul (魂).
[124] "A wall of dung cannot be repaired, deadwood cannot be carved (朽木糞土)." Gongyechang, 公冶長," *Analects*. Confucius' words to his disciple Jaeyŏ (宰予 Zaiyu), who was napping—i.e., there is no way to teach a lazy man.

was Chinbaek's warning.[125]
In the olden days, strong-willed people
were ashamed of sleepiness, right?
Besides, you're a promising scholar,
blessed with many innate gifts and a strong body.
Your zeal for poetry and books is hot as burning coal,
and you're sorry that time flies by like a stream.
You think nothing of leaning against the mud wall
and sleeping on a grass mat.
You're the wick of a blue oil lamp
and the desk of yellow books.[126]
You don't care about heat and cold
and burning the lamp from year to year.
But many devils make mischief because your dan[127] is about to turn circular,
Yach'as[128] envy you because your Zen meditation is about to break through.
When your studies are about to ripen,
snake-like sleep will instantly come over you;
your studying will wane,
your will collapse.
Therefore I pitied you
and tried to open a hole of wisdom
with a needle in your crown[129]
to bring you back.
I intended no harm,
only to wake you up.

---

[125] 陳柏 Chenbai's suxingyemei 夙興夜寐 is a warning to rise early in the morning and go to sleep late at night—i.e., to work hard.
[126] A hard-working scholar's life.
[127] 丹 dan: The energy of life in Taoism. If you have this, you will be an ascetic and become immortal.
[128] 夜叉, yaksa in Sanskrit. A male demon in Buddhism.
[129] The phrase means to admonish.

The prick of my needle feels like an awn of sorghum stinging
 you.
Its mark is like a fresh-cut cherry blossom.
The itching and scratching are merely inconveniences,
not a calamity, boil, or scar.
No one embroiders unless the cloth is silk,
no one grinds unless the stone is jade.
The decorated children of the noblemen in the capital
grew up in a warm house,
their souls were indulged in loose living among the scarlet skirts,
their bones soaked in golden wine cups.
Because they mistake the dream world for their home
and worship the devil of sleep as their elder brother,
they don't respond
even if their crowns are stung and backs struck.
I don't want to help them even a little.
I'm not stingy with you,
I'm generous. So why
do you regard my virtue as a vice
and repay my favor with atrocity?
You're eccentric, like Hanso,[130]
your writing is like bantering, in the style of Ut'ong.[131]
How could you hurt me
so badly last night?
A man of great virtue cut out his own flesh
to feed a hungry tiger.[132]

---

[130] 韓昭 Hanzhao: An official in the Former Shu, famous for his eccentricities and skill at flattery.
[131] 尤侗 Yu Dong: A famous poet and opera composer of the late Ming and early Qing dynasties.
[132] In *Zhuangzi*, there is a story that Danbao (單豹), a virtuous man in the Lu dynasty, lived in a rock cave and drank only water. Because he did not pursue worldly fame or profit, he remained baby-faced even at the age of seventy. But a hungry tiger killed and ate him.

A nobleman even rebuked a woman
for foolishly killing a louse.[133]
Ancient philosophers were merciful
and regarded things and their selves as the same.
I'm not sure if it's wise
to compare the present to the past.
When a dog scares off a thief,
people give it minced meat;
when a cat keeps mice away,
people share their blanket.
But they don't care
for much greater things.
You have too little knowledge
to appreciate this,
and I'm ashamed of you
for reproaching me.
I will leave now
and never come back."
The color of his face changed
as he prepared to leave.
"Ah, now I can see.
Please don't go away
but waken me from my dullness with your needle."
I rose to reward him
and woke with a yawn
only to find this, too, was a dream.

---

[133] The allusion to this story is unknown.

Ode on a Mother Who Delivered Her Fifth Son

There was a mother with four sons near Kyŏnggŭmja's house.

Hearing that she had delivered another baby,
I asked if it was another boy.
She rose from her bed after seven days;
the swelling in her face had yet to subside.
Without any sign of joy,
she sighed, leaning against the doorpost.

When I sent my maid servant to congratulate her, she said in anger,

"I don't even have time to worry—
why do you annoy us with your congratulations?"

I thought she behaved like this out of embarrassment. So I said with a laugh,

"You delivered your fifth son—
how can you not be happy?"

She said,

"Government officials will be happy
because a soldier has been added to the district.
How can I be happy to have a son
when there is no money in this poor house?"

Thinking this strange, I asked again why she was so angry. She said,

"Heaven is already my enemy,

even ghosts don't help me.
My naked house has nothing,
overflowing with children.
I haven't failed to deliver one every three years,
now I have two pairs plus one.
My oldest son barely plows the field,
the second one just carries fodder for the cow.
Each of the others with their drooping hair
empties a bowl of boiled barley.
Subjects must do compulsory labor
and duty follows such work:
Sumi,[134] Poin,[135]
Sogo,[136] and Apyŏng.[137]
The navy is most important,
and they are strict about recruiting.
When a male baby is three months old,
the village headman reports his name.
He is taken in swaddling clothes to the government office
and immediately entered into the army registry.
In autumn, the petty officials meet
to press us to pay the tax;
they stand in front of the gate with angry faces,
sounding like a tiger with its cub.
The tax for the bigger boy is two hundred chŏn,[138]
fifty for the smaller one.
If we don't pay the tax on the morning of the designated day

---

[134] 需米, an adult on the military registry in the Chosŏn dynasty who paid a grain tax instead of serving on active duty.
[135] 保布, an adult who paid a military cloth tax instead of serving on active duty.
[136] 束伍, a regimental troop in the late Chosŏn dynasty.
[137] 牙兵, a troop under the direct command of a general in the late Chosŏn dynasty.
[138] A traditional unit of money.

they will arrest us and take us to the government office.
Thus we bake salt until sunset
and work the plough all year long.
Hungry as we are, we don't even eat a grain,
nor wear so much as a thread in the cold
in order to prepare the military cloth tax,
or else we can't meet the deadline.
Shoeless, standing on the ice,
we shed tears helplessly.
Considering all this,
how can a baby be precious?
Babies are cheap—
that's why I'm sad."

I felt sorry for her and tried to console her with old stories:

"Ah, perhaps you don't know
that in the Han and Tang periods
there were lots of wars.
They selected armored soldiers from every household
and recruited border guards from every family.
They drove them like tigers and wild oxen
and threatened them with spears and axes
so they wouldn't dream of going home
to become peaceful bones after they died.
To think about it even now
makes my hair stand on end.
But now you're living in the world of the Yao and Shun era[139]
and peace has prevailed for a hundred years;
the nation doesn't talk of war.
No one knows anything about military weapons.

---

[139] Refers to the peaceful era in which Emperor Yao and Emperor Shun ruled the world with virtue.

They live their own lives,
playing with little children, raising grandchildren.
To judge the present against the past—
there used to be trouble in the mud and now there is glory in the clouds.
Is there any reason to be upset
over a little military tax."

She said,

"No, it isn't so. At that time, if one succeeded,
his face would have been painted on the Kirin'gak.[140]
If one failed, his bones were found in Yongsa.[141]
But they didn't shed tears
worrying about money.
I think today's sorrow
is greater than in the past."

She stopped weeping, then went on with a sigh.

I pity the sufferings of the people,
and lament the disagreeable military service tax.
I record this dialogue and write this ode
for the future collector of folk tales.

---

[140] 麒麟閣, A royal palace built by Emperor Wuwei in the Han dynasty. Portraits of the eleven vassals of merit were hung there.
[141] Refers to the wild desert near the northern border of China.

Afterword[142]

I passed the Chinsa Examination[143] in 1792. I studied the Kongnyŏngbyŏllyŏ style[144] of writing that fall, living with Maesa Yi Kisang in Kim Ŭng'il's annex house in Western Panch'on. Morning and evening, I wrote short odes whenever I found time, dozens in imitation of Kangŏm[145] and P'ojo,[146] and dozens more in the style of Ku Yangsu[147] and Sosik.[148] These I collected into a book, which I kept in my bookcase.

I was exiled to Yŏngsŏng[149] in 1797, implicated in the major criminal case of canards.[150] I was arrested again and sent

---

[142] This afterword was written by Yi Ok's friend, Kim Ryŏ, who compiled and edited his works.
[143] A primary literary licensing examination for government office.
[144] An elaborate style of writing poetry practiced by students for the national examination, in which a pair of four-character lines and six-character lines is repeated.
[145] 江淹 Jiang Yan, a literary figure and politician in the Liang dynasty, famous for his odes.
[146] 鮑照, Baozhao, a literary figure in the Song dynasty, who composed many outstanding odes.
[147] 歐陽脩, Ouyang Xiu, a Northern Song period writer, historian, and politician. His prose style is plain and natural; his odes depict in a dynamic fashion human and non-human things, extending the possibilities of this traditional form; his masterpiece, "Ch'usŏngbu" (秋聲賦, "Ode on an Autumnal Sound"), enacts the decay of the ten thousand things of the world in the sound of the autumn wind.
[148] 蘇軾, Su shi, a writer, politician, and artist of the Northern Song dynasty, regarded as the greatest poet of the Song dynasty. His masterpiece, "Chŏkpyŏkpu" (赤壁賦, Chibi bu, Ode on a Red Cliff), marries landscape and emotion in a dexterous fashion.
[149] Another name of Puryŏng.
[150] A major criminal case of canards about the spreading of Catholicism in Korea during the reign of Chŏngjo and Sunjo; rumors

to Chinhae in 1801. When I finally returned from exile in 1806, a lifetime's worth of writings was gone. Last year, Ut'ae, Kisang's son, asked me to edit his father's posthumous works. There I found drafts of my miscellaneous odes. Kisang must be happy to have such a wonderful son. I thought of his life and death again, tears filling my eyes unawares. I picked them out to copy.

Tam'ong[151] wrote this on the next day of Tano,[152] in the spring of 1819.

---

of the advent of the True Man and some Confucian scholars' plans to sail to the Island were in the air.

[151] Another penname of Kim Ryŏ.

[152] The festival on the fifth day of the fifth month of the lunar calendar.

Plain Verses[153]

---

[153] Iŏn 俚諺: Refers to vulgar words or proverbs used by common people.

First Difficulty

Someone asked, "Why did you write plain verses? Why didn't you follow the example of kukp'ung,[154] akpu,[155] or sagok[156] instead of writing plain verses?"

I replied, "I didn't do this voluntarily, I was ordered to do it. How can I write kukp'ung, akpu, and sagok and not plain verses? If you study how kukp'ung became kukp'ung, akpu became akpu, and sagok became neither kukp'ung nor akpu but sagok, you will see I had no choice but to write plain verses."

He said, "So kukp'ungs, akpus, sagoks, and your plain verses were not written by their authors?"

I replied, "How dare writers think they write by themselves? The being who made them writes them into reality. Who is this being? All the things of the world. They have their own nature, images, colors, and voices. When you see them in their totality, all creation is one. But when you see them in detail, each and every thing in the world is also a creation in and of itself. The fallen flowers in the windy forest are scattered about like rainfall. But if you discriminate among them, red flowers are red and white flowers are white. The heavenly music sounds like a thunder, but if you listen

---

[154] Guofeng 國風: The folk music of the locals in ancient China or "Tunes from the States," a section of the *Shijing* 詩經, a collection of Chinese poems circa 1000 to 600 BCE, containing poems from fifteen states in northern China.

[155] Yuefu 樂府: The songs collected and composed by the Music Bureau during the reign of Emperor Wu in the Han dynasty or the poems written in that style.

[156] Siqu 詞曲: Refers to song lyrics composed during the mid-Tang era and popular in the Song dynasty and folk songs popular in the Yuan dynasty.

carefully string music is string music, and pipe music is pipe music. Each has its own color and voice."

A poem exists in manuscript, in nature, already complete, before people draw eight trigrams[157] and devise sŏkye.[158] Which is why writers of kukp'ung, akpu, and sagok cannot claim to write their poems by themselves, and why they cannot quote another's work. Creation reveals images in writers' dreams, which are represented in the ki[159] constellation to communicate emotion.

Thus when the work becomes a poem through the person chosen to be its channel, it enters his ears and eyes as water flows, stays above the lower part of the belly, and emerges through his mouth and fingertips. The poem is not created by his subjective will. It is like Sakyamuni accidently entering into the peacock's belly through its mouth, and then coming out after a while through its buttocks. I am not certain whether Sakyamuni is Sakyamuni or Sakyamuni is the peacock. Therefore a writer is the translator of the whole of creation as well as its painter.

When a translator translates Na Hach'u's[160] words, the language is Pukpŏn;[161] if he translates Matteo Ricci's[162] words, the language is a Western language. Even though its sounds are unfamiliar to you, you should not change or correct them. When a painter draws an image of someone, if he paints Maeng

---

[157] Bagua 八卦: Eight symbols invented by Fuxi 伏羲氏. These symbols represent the fundamental principles of reality.
[158] Qixie 書契: The characters of ancient China carved on trees or strings knotted together.
[159] Ji 箕: One of the twenty-eight Mansions of the Chinese constellations.
[160] Naghachu 納哈出 (?~1388): An ethnic Mongol leader and general of the Yuan dynasty.
[161] Beifan 北蕃: A Country of Jurchens.
[162] Matteo Ricci (1552-1610): An Italian Jesuit missionary who worked in Ming China.

Sanggun,[163] it becomes a small image; if he draws Kŏ Mup'ae,[164] the image will resemble Chang Chŏk.[165] Though his shape is different from that of a commoner, you should not imagine the shape and draw it on the canvas. How can it be different?

Generally speaking, ten thousand things are ten thousand things, and therefore cannot be reduced to one. Even the sky is not the same throughout the day, the earth is different from one place to another. It's like ten million people have ten million different names, and three hundred days have three hundred different works. It cannot be otherwise.

If you review the historical record, each nation, including Xia, Yin, Zhou, Han, Jin, Song, Qi, Liang, Chen, Sui, Tang Song, and Yuan, is unique, each has its own poetry. Likewise various countries of the world, such as Zhou, Zhao, Bei, Yong, Wei, Zheng, Qi, Wei, Tang, Qin, and Chen, are different from one another, each with its own poetry. Generations change every thirty years, customs are different if you travel one hundred li. How can someone born during the reign of King Qianlong (1735-1795) and living in Hanyang,[166] Chosŏn, speak so foolishly about writing kukp'ung, akpu, and sagok, craning your short neck, forcibly opening wide your narrow eyes?

This is what I have seen with my own eyes—which is why I know that writing poetry cannot be done by artificial means.

---

[163] Meng Changjun 孟嘗君: A prime minister of the Qi dynasty. A small man, he was one of the four famous figures in the Warring States period.

[164] Ju Wuba 巨無覇: A person who lived in Han China. He was ten ch'ŏk tall (about ten feet, three meters) and so heavy that a horse couldn't pull the cart when he was in it; even three horses couldn't carry him.

[165] Chang Di 長狄: A northern tribe in the Spring and Autumn period. They were said to be one hundred ch'ŏk tall (about one hundred feet, thirty meters).

[166] 漢陽: The capital of Chosŏn, the old name of Seoul.

The everlasting creation never missed showing itself even for a day during the reign of King Qianlong; the joyous things of the world never missed a beat under Hanyang. Stupid as I am, I'm grateful for the fact that my ears, eyes, mouth, and hands are the same as those of ancient people. This is why I cannot help but write poems—and why I write only plain verses, not kukp'ungs like "Toyo" and "Kaltam,"[167] akpus like "Churo" and Sabiong,"[168] sagoks like "Ch'ogyŏngyohong" and "Chŏmnyŏnhwa."[169] How did I choose this? How is this what I do?

What shames me is that I am so inferior to the ancients in letting all of creation express itself and move through me. It must be my fault. This is why I call many rhyming plain verses not kukp'ung, akpu, and sagok but i (vulgar) and ŏn (demotic): to apologize to creation.

A butterfly flying past a cold and emaciated Hangnyŏng chrysanthemum asks, "Why are you yellow, not the white of a Japanese apricot, the red of a peony, or the red-and-white of a peach and damson?" Hangnyŏng replies, "How did I make it so? Time did it. And what can I do about Time?"

Why do you ask me the same question as the butterfly?

---

[167] Taoyao 桃夭 and Getan 葛覃 are pieces in *The Book of Odes*.
[168] Both Zhulu 朱鷺 and Sbeiweng 思悲翁 are akpus of the Han dynasty.
[169] Both Zhuyingyaohong 燭影搖紅 and "Dielianhua 蝶戀花" are sagoks.

Second Difficulty

Someone asked, "You say that all of creation entered you and came out as plain verses. Then why are your ten thousand things limited to only one or two things? Why do your plain verses mention only such things of woman as wearing powder and rouge, skirts and decorative hairpins? The ancients said you shouldn't hear something if it isn't proper, you shouldn't look at something if it isn't proper, and you shouldn't speak of something if it isn't proper. So why did you do that?"

I sprang to my feet, then knelt down and said in gratitude, "Your teaching sounds profound. I realize my error. Please burn this immediately. But I beseech you to instruct me to the very end. I dare to ask, what kind of book is *Sijŏn?*"[170]

"It's a classic."

"Who wrote it?"

"The writers of the time"

"Who selected them?"

"Confucius."

"Who annotated them?"

"Chuja[171] made the variorum edition, and the Confucian scholars of Han China added notes for each poem."

"What is their core meaning?"

"Samusa,[172] that is, no evil thoughts in thinking."

"What use are they?"

"To teach people how to practice the good."

---

[170] Refers to *Shichuan* 詩傳, an explication of *The Book of Odes*.

[171] Zhuzi 朱子: A Song dynasty calligrapher, historian, philosopher, poet, and politician.

[172] Siwuxie 思無邪. The Master (Confucius) said: "There are three hundred songs in *The Book of Songs*, but his one phrase tells it all: thoughts never twisty." *The Four Chinese Classics: Tao Te Ching, Chuang Tzu, Analects, Mencius*, translated and with commentary by David Hinton. Counterpoint, 2013.

"What are the so-called Chunam[173] and Sonam?"[174]
"Kukp'ung."
"What are they about"
After a while, he replied, "Most of them are about the things of women."
"How many works are there in total?"
"Eleven in Chunam and fourteen in Sonam."
"How many works do not portray the things of women?"
"Five in total, including 'T'ojŏ' and 'Kamdang.'"[175]
"Is that so? It's really strange! Is it the same from ancient times that all of creation lies in the things of women, like wearing powder and rouge, and putting on skirts and decorative hairpins? Why do you think the old poets said that? Do you think they disliked the proverb that you shouldn't see, listen, and speak of something if it isn't proper? Dear guest! Are you willing to listen to my explanation? There must be some reason for this."

When you observe all of creation, nothing is more important than observing people. When you observe people, nothing is more important than observing their emotions. And nothing is truer than observing the emotions between men and women. My body exists because there is a world, and this thing exists because there is my body, and this emotion exists because of this thing. By observing this thing you can know the good and evil in a heart, whether someone is wise or not, whether something is profitable or detrimental, whether a custom is extravagant or frugal, whether the land is thick or thin, whether a house will prosper or decline, whether a nation is orderly or chaotic, and whether the age is prosperous or in decline.

As far as human emotion is concerned, people pretend to be happy in unhappy situations, pretend to be angry when they

---

[173] Zhounan 周南: One of the fifteen Guefeng in *The Book of Odes*.
[174] Zhaonan 召南: One of the fifteen Guefeng in *The Book of Odes*.
[175] "Tuju 兔罝" and "Gantang" 甘棠

shouldn't be angry, pretend to be sad when they shouldn't be sad, pretend or wish to be joyful, to love or hate, when they shouldn't be joyful, or love and hate. It is really difficult to judge what is true or false. The emotions between men and women are the fundamental things of life, as well as the natural way of the Universe.

When people hold a wedding ceremony and light the honeymoon candle, ask after the other's health and make deep bows, these are sincere emotions. Sincere also to argue fiercely and scold the mirror stand in the boudoir, to wait in tears under the beaded hanging screen or on the balustrade, to miss someone in a dream, to sell one's smile and song for gold and gems in the red-light district, to love pillows embroidered with a pair of mandarin ducks, jade-colored silk comforters, and rosy cheeks, to beat jade-colored silk with fulling sticks on a frosty night, or brood over sad things and soothe resentments under the lamplight on a rainy night, or give jade jewelry in the shade of flowers under moonlight and then to steal the fragrance.[176]

In every case, these kinds of sincere emotions are not fake. Modest and chaste, when they are reached in the right Way, they are true emotions in and of themselves; rude, prejudiced, lazy, or arrogant, having gone astray from the right Way, they are still "true" in their own way. The former should be followed, the latter taken as warnings. Because they are true, people can follow them. Because they are true, people can be warned.

This is why we study emotions—the heart, the thing, the custom, the land, the house, the nation, the age. Better to observe the world through the emotions of men and women.

This is why there are twenty poems apiece about relations between men and women in Chunam and Sonam, thirty-seven

---

[176] The phrase is a metaphor for a man and a woman having a secret affair.

out of thirty-nine in Wip'ung,[177] sixteen of the twenty-one in Chŏngp'ung.[178] This is also why those poets took the trouble to look, listen, and speak about what wasn't proper; why our greatest sage, Kongbuja,[179] selected these poems; why Confucian scholars like Mos,[180] Chŏng Hyŏn,[181] and Chayang[182] added notes and published variorum editions; why you told me the poems contain no evil thoughts and thus are suitable for teaching the practice of the good.

So why don't you know that listening to what is improper is not listening to what will become proper, since what is improper is not to see what will become proper, and speaking about what is improper is not to talk about what will become proper? Besides, it isn't true that what people see, listen, and say isn't always proper.

So I say that chŏngp'ung[183] and ŭmp'ung[184] are not poetry but *The Spring and Autumn Annals.*[185] Novels of manners like

---

[177] Weifeng 衛風: One of the fifteen Guofeng in *The Book of Odes*. There are actually ten poems in Wip'ung; thirty-nine seems to be an error introduced in the process of copying.

[178] Zhengfeng 鄭風: One of the fifteen Guofeng in *The Book of Odes*.

[179] Kung Fu-tse 孔夫子: Refers to Confucius 孔子.

[180] Maos 毛氏: Refers to the scholars Mao Heng 毛亨 and his brother Mao Zedong 毛萇 of the early Han dynasty. Mao Heng was the author of *The Ancient Poetry of Mao Shi* 詩詁訓傳 and gave it to Mao Zedong. Mao Shi is another name for *The Book of Odes*.

[181] Zheng Xuan 鄭玄: A great Confucian scholar from the end of the Han dynasty.

[182] Refers to Zhu Xi, because he built the Ziyang School 紫陽書堂 to teach students.

[183] zhengfeng 正風:

[184] yinfeng 淫風: Originally an obscene custom between a man and a woman, but here it refers to the love poems in wip'ung and chŏngp'ung.

[185] 春秋: One of the Five Classics and the official history of the Lu dynasty compiled by Confucius.

Kŭmpyŏngmae[186] and *Yukp'odan*[187] cannot be designated as erotic literature. If you look into a writer's heart, there is no reason to think he cannot write about what can be classified as chŏngp'ung and ŭmp'ung. What do you think? But there is one more thing to consider.

A woman has an eccentric character. Her joy, melancholy, resentment, and coquetry flow naturally from her emotions, as if she keeps needles on the tip of her tongue and makes fun of the axe by lifting an eyebrow. For a poetic subject nothing is more mysterious than a woman. A woman is an uncanny being. Her attitude, words, attire, and dwelling know no limit. It is like hearing the song of a Chinese oriole during a nap or enjoying peach blossoms while drunk. No other person can be as rich a poetic subject as a woman.

Alas! Though a woman is rich and mysterious, if the person who writes about her wandering leisurely around the phoenix lake, intoxicated by the sound of pipes and drum—how can he reach that state of being? If he lives on a blue mountain, hangs out with monkeys, and communicates with cranes, how can he reach that state? If he is devoted to natural sciences and recites nature's beauty, how can he reach that state? If he is sunk into a

---

[186] *Jin Ping Mei* (金瓶梅), translated into English as *The Plum in the Golden Vase* or *The Golden Lotus*, was a novel of manners composed in the vernacular during the late Ming dynasty (1368–1644). *Jin Ping Mei* takes its name from the three central female characters — Pan Jinlian (潘金蓮, "Golden Lotus"); Li Ping'er (李瓶兒, "Little Vase"), a concubine of Ximen Qing; and Pang Chunmei (龐春梅 "Spring Plum Blossoms"), a young maid who rose to power within the family.

[187] *Rouputuan* 肉蒲團 is a 17th-century Chinese erotic novel published under a pseudonym usually attributed to Li Yu (李漁). It portrays in intimate detail sexual relationships between a young talented student Wei Yangsheng(未央生) and his six partners.

wine jar, brandishes his brush, and sing songs, intoxicated by flowers and willows, how can he reach that state?

My present state is neither this nor that. But this is a good world: the spring landscape is peaceful, people merrily come and go, and in the city glittering as if covered with silk, people are busy and noisy. As for the man? He leads a leisurely life, after practicing frugality for years with ink and brush. When he wanders the streets in daylight he encounters men and women; when he returns home in the evening he finds on his desk only a few books. His mind itches as if a thousand lice are moving in his liver. Only after I have vomited up all of them can I quit.

If I have to write a poem, how can I ignore the mysterious, rich, and truest emotions in all of creation? Do you understand? Do you hear me? I think the writer of kukp'ung was thousands of times more gifted than me. But his goal in writing was not much different than mine.

Third Difficulty

Someone said I was presumptuous, ill-tempered, and provincial, because I didn't use the original names for well-known or obscure things like clothes, food, and containers, but used the vernacular.

I replied, "You're right. As you said, I have long violated the law, naming my house after my name instead of "Agyangnu"[188] or "Ch'wiongjŏng."[189] When I turned fifteen, I celebrated my coming of age and was given my adult and other name. But I didn't take my adult or other name from the ancients. Because I took them from my own name, I have long broken the law. But I am not alone in this. You are also guilty. Why do you keep your surname instead of Huang Di's Ji[190] or Wang and Xie of the Jin dynasty, Cui and Lu of the Tang dynasty?"[191]

The man laughed. "I talked about the names of things, but why are you ridiculously talking about the names of people?"

I replied, "Then I will talk about the names of things, which are too many to count, but about the names of things we can see. The ancient Chinese called that mat woven out of cogongrass sŏk (席 xi), but we call it totchari (兜單席). The ancient Chinese called the wooden rack on which they put an oil lamp tŭnggyŏng (燈檠 dēngqíng), but we call it kangmyông (光明). The ancient Chinese called what people bound animal hairs to make pointed p'il (筆 bi) but we call it put (賦詩). They call

---

[188] Yueyanglou 岳陽樓: Yueyang Tower is an ancient Chinese tower in Yueyang, Hunan Province, on the shore of Lake Dongting.
[189] Zuiwengting 醉翁亭: Zuiweng Pavilion is near Chuzhou City, Anhui, China.
[190] Yellow Emperor (黃帝), a legendary ancient Chinese emperor, who moved to Jishui (姬水) and thus changed his family name to Ji (姬).
[191] The surnames of the most famous family in the Six dynasties and the Tang dynasty.

the whitish paste made from pounded paper mulberry zhi (紙), but we call it chong'i (照意). They took names from what they called things, and we take names from what we call things."

Who knows whether what they call things are the real names of things or what we call things are their real names. They did not call xi 席 or dengqing 燈檠, because Pangushi[192] 盤古氏 named things by royal order when he took office. Thus they are not their original names. What we call put 賦詩 or chong'i 照意 are not the names given to them by the real parents of the mulberry tree or of animal hair. All the names they used and we use are the same in that they are not their original names. They named things according to what they deemed appropriate, and we do the same. So how can we throw away our names and follow theirs? And how they can throw away their names and follow ours?

A local governor once asked an official to go to the market to buy food and other stuff for an ancestral rite. The official bought everything on the list, but he could not figure out what pŏpyu 法油 was. The oil merchant said "I have only two kinds of oil, sesame and lamp. There is no oil called pŏpyu." The official came back without pŏpyu, because he did not know that pŏpyu is lamp oil. This must be the fault of the local governor, not the official or the oil merchant.

A certain man living in Seoul once said to a country person: "Please visit me because ch'ŏngp'o 青泡 (green-lentil jelly) in the market looks delicious. I will treat you to your heart's content." The person thought this must be very rare and visited his house the next day. But the Seoulite gave him green tofu. Jelly is called green tofu among the townspeople. The country man went home angry and said to his wife, "The Seoulite cheated me today. I didn't know what kind of food ch'ŏngp'o is, but I visited his house because he said he would treat me. He did not prepare any

---

[192] The creator of the universe in Chinese mythology.

ch'ŏngp'o but gave me only jelly." He did not calm down for a long time. Nor did he ever realize that ch'ŏngp'o is jelly. This, then, is the fault of the Seoulite, not the country person. I wonder how many poets in our country would be unable to buy lamp oil, and how many people eat ch'ŏngp'o without knowing that it is jelly.

By the stream there is a bird called ch'ŏlchak 鐵雀, because it has beautiful blue feathers. There is an old poem that says, "The jade-colored bird sings in the country house thick with bamboo trees." But what does the tribute of Wŏlsang have to do with the country house in Chosŏn?[193] There is a bird that cries sadly at night, so it is called chŏptong. There is also an old poem that says, "I cannot bear the sound of the cuckoo in this region." But what does the soul of P'ach'ok[194] have to do with the land of Chosŏn? These kinds of things are too numerous to ignore.

If we name things like clothes, food, and containers as we call them, even a three-year-old will have no difficulty understanding them. But when one grips a brush to write on paper the record of people or things he looks to his right and left and asks people around him the names of things, not knowing what Chinese names correspond to the things. How does this happen?

Ah, I think I know why. They say "local names are what locals use. We can only say them but can't write them with a brush." I don't know why the Silla named their country Sŏrabŏl 徐那伐 rather than Kyŏng 京? And why they use Isagŭm instead of Ch'imun as the title for a king. Why did they use Pak instead

---

[193] Yuechang 越裳: The historic name of an ethnic group in southern China, Myanmar, and India.
[194] Bashu 巴蜀 : The area of Sichuan, originally the two provinces of Qin and Han.

of Ho for the king's surname? How could Kim Pusik[195] forget to write it down?

How did the yoga[196] of Han and *Kŭmpyŏngmae*, a novel of manners, express themselves so gracefully that even people in foreign countries know the names of these things? Was it because Maesŭng[197] and Sama Sangyŏ[198] liked the grotesque and Pongju[199] was provincial?

Alas! If the names of things like xí 席, dengqing 燈檠, bi 筆, and zhi 紙 are appropriate, I'll discard my idea. Nor will I insist like someone who has to win every argument that we only use local words. But when people call blue feathers a jade-colored bird and the sad moan the cry of a cuckoo, I will not buy pŏpyu and eat ch'ŏngp'o, even if I am forced to write Hangŭl poems because of my meager talent and dull tongue. How can I refrain from using local words?

It is regrettable that Ch'anghil[200] or Chuhwang[201] didn't invent characters for us earlier—and that Tan'gun or Kija didn't use letters to teach words. Many local words are not named in letters—is that why I fear naming things in letters? This is why I

---

[195] 金富軾 (107~1151) A Koryŏ period calligrapher, military general, philosopher, poet, and politician, best known as the author of 三國史記 (The Record of Three Kingdoms) in 1145.

[196] Naoge 鐃歌 : Originally a military song, but here it refers to "Eighteen Works of Naoge."

[197] Mei Cheng 枚乘 (?-140 BCE) A Western Han poet who composed in fu 賦 style, author of Seven Stimuli 七发 .

[198] Sima Xiangru 司馬相如: a Western Han dynasty poet, one of the greatest composers of fu.

[199] Fengzhou 凰州: Refers to Wang Shizen 王世貞 (1526 – 1590), a Ming dynasty writer-politician. Fengzhou was his penname.

[200] Cang Xie 蒼頡: A legendary figure said to have invented letters, imitating bird and animal tracks.

[201] Zhu Huang 朱皇 : He seems to have worked with Cang Xie to invent letters, but details about him are unknown.

use local names. Am I doing this because I am provincial? Or because I am eccentric and presumptuous?

You said I'm arrogant, so I will speak in a loud voice without fear of being arrogant. I found in Kanghŭijajŏn[202] that nūk 玏 is "the name of the Korean royal family," along with tap 畓, which means "a rice paddy for the Korean people." Wu Changju's[203] akpus often mentioned our country's local words. One day you will see. Someone in China will collect words; after recording the names of the things I invented, he will note that "these were coined by Kyŏnggŭmja of Chosŏn." Ha ha!

---

[202] *Kangxi Zidian*: The standard Chinese dictionary published in 1716. Emperor Kangxi of the Qing dynasty ordered its compilation.
[203] You Changzhou: Refers to You Tong 尤侗 (1618~1704), a Qing dynasty writer and literary critic whose hometown was Changzhou.

Graceful Rhymes

The graceful (雅) is permanent and right. Rhyme is melody. For example, it is right and permanent for a wife to love her husband, be thrifty in housekeeping, and diligent in her work. This section is called Graceful Rhymes, and portrays love, respect, thrift, and diligence. It is composed of seventeen poems.

1.
My husband holds wooden geese[204]
and I lift up a dry pheasant.[205]
May the love between two people know no limit
until the pheasant cries and the geese fly off.

2.
With a blessed hand, I lift a red-threaded cup,[206]
the nuptial drink for my husband.
May you have three sons with the first cup
and enjoy a long life of ninety years with the third one.

3.
My husband comes riding on a white horse

---

[204] In a traditional wedding ceremony the groom delivers a pair of wooden geese to the person in charge of the wedding for the bride. These geese represent the bride and groom, because they keep the same partner for life and never look for another, even if one dies; hence the wooden geese symbolize fidelity.
[205] In the wedding ceremony the bride makes a deep bow and offers dried pheasant or chicken to her in-laws, a gift representing fertility.
[206] In the wedding ceremony the bride and groom share wine, the first drink signifying their tie as a couple, the second, drunk in a gourd cup, their unity. The gourd cup is tied with red and blue threads.

and I go to his house in a red palanquin.
In front of the gate my mother says,
"Be careful when you bow to your in-laws."

4.
My house is near the Kwangt'ong Bridge
and my husband's house is in Sujinbang.
Whenever I ride in the palanquin,
tears fall and splash on my skirt.

5.
When we linked our black hairs,
we pledged to live together until they turn gray.
Though I did nothing shameful, I was too shy
to talk to him for three months.

6.
I have long practiced the court style of writing
but the letter "o" is a little angular.
My in-laws, pleased with my writings,
call me a great female scholar of the Korean alphabet.

7.
I rise at three and comb my hair
to go ask after my in-law's health at five.
When I go home to my parents,
I will not eat and sleep until noon.

8.
My silkworms have grown to the size of a palm
And I go outside to pick mulberry leaves.
Nor am I without Eastern Sea silk.
I raise silkworms as a hobby.

9.
As I sew clothes for my beloved,
the fragrance of flowers makes me drowsy.
I spin the needle and pin it to the collar,
then sit to read *A Tale of Sukhyang*.[207]

10.
My mother-in-law gave me a pair
of jade figures as a wedding gift.
Unable to say I want to wear them,
I wrap them in an embroidered cloth.[208]

11.
Through the window a girl servant calls
"Lady" in a soft voice:
"They say they will send you a palanquin tomorrow
if you can't stop thinking about your maiden home."

12.
With green Sangsa silk[209] and two needles,
I made an ear-shaped pouch,
which I folded into a three-layered butterfly shape
and lifted my hand to give to my beloved.

---

[207] This novel was one of the most famous and widely read in the late Chosŏn period, especially among women. It portrays a female protagonist, Sukhyang, who was born into a noble family and orphaned during a riot, then adopted by a noble family. She suffered many hardships until she found her true love, with whom she led a happy life before ascending to heaven with him. There are more than eighty different versions of the book, which is used as a textbook by Japanese translators learning Korean.

[208] Yuso (流蘇): Cloth embroidered with tassels.

[209] Sangsadan (相思緞): A thin green silk. Because "sangsa" means thinking of the beloved, it is used to make clothes for the beloved.

13.
Most people love to swing,
But I don't like to join them.
I excuse myself, saying my arms are weak,
but I fear that my jade dragon hairpin will fall off.

14.
My husband's clothes dried in the deep night.
After wrapping them in a pretty cloth decorated
with a sun pattern, I keep them in a bamboo basket.
The fragrance lingers on my hands and his clothes.

15.
I wash my jade-like hands again
and remove some of my flowery cosmetics.
The day for ancestral rites is coming,
I take off my red skirt for a while.

16.
We have a crimson futon mattress with flowery patterns
and a dark blue silk comforter.
They don't need to be made of silk with cloud patterns[210]
and embroidered with four golden turtles.

17.
People take silk clothes lightly
but I cherish even rough cotton clothes.[211]
Farmers hoed in dry fields
and women wove in poor houses to produce them.

---

[210] Unmundan (雲文緞): A fine silk cloth with cloud patterns, usually used at the royal court.
[211] Pobyŏngŭi (步兵衣): A rough, thick cotton cloth used for the uniforms of popyŏng (foot soldiers).

Beautiful Rhymes

The beautiful (艶) is what is splendid. This section portrays what is arrogant, luxurious, frivolous, and too polished. It does not reach for the graceful nor descend to the libertine; hence the beautiful. It is composed of eighteen poems.

1.
Don't plant the Ullŭng peach tree—[212]
it won't match my new makeup.
Don't snap the drooping willows—[213]
my long eyelashes are better.

2.
You said you're coming from the pub—
which I know is the whorehouse.
Why is blush like a flower
imprinted on your summer linen jacket?

3.
I will not go to Pyŏkchang-dong,[214]

---

[212] There is a record in *The Annals of King Sejong* that peaches produced in Ullŭng Island were as big as gourds. They were regarded as the best peaches in the markets in Seoul in the late Chosŏn period.
[213] A drooping willow is used as a metaphor for the eyelashes of a beautiful woman. See Wang Wei's 「送人使安西」: "渭城朝雨浥輕塵, 客舍青青柳色新. 勸君更盡一杯酒, 西出陽關無故人." "A spring rain in the morning wets the light dust, and the green willows around the guest house are extraordinarily fresh. Old friend invites you to drink another farewell to the bar. After leaving Yangguan West Road, there will be no old friends anymore." (https://fanti.dugushici.com/mingju/928)
[214] A village in Songhyŏn-dong, Sagan-dong, and Chunghak-dong, known for its brothels.

wearing white socks that look like cucumber seeds.
The sewing servants[215] who create new fashions
will make fun of me.

4.
What do I have on my head?
A bamboo joint hair pin that looks like a flying butterfly.
What do I have on my feet?
Silk shoes that look like opened flowers.

5.
My slip is made of red sheer silk,[216]
my outer skirt, indigo silk.
Whenever I take a step, the silver peach trinket
and fragrant eggplant trinket collide: *clink, clink*.

6.
At other times, my arm becomes flabby as milk
after I put up my peach hair and apply makeup.
But today, after putting on the bridal headpiece,
I should have painted rouge and powder earlier.

7.
I made an appointment with an old woman, my eastern neighbor,
and crossed at the Norang port the next morning.
Fearing that once again I might not bear a son,
I visit the shrine of the harvest god[217] to ask for help.

---

[215] Female servants who sewed in the Royal Clothing Office. They usually worked as gisaengs.
[216] A thin silk mainly used for summer clothes. Its original meaning is silk from Hangzhou.
[217] One of many gods worshipped by a shaman, who blesses parents and presides over the harvest.

8.
Unable to wait until the garden balsam opened its flowers,
I dyed my fingernails with its leaves.
I always worried my fingernails would be green,
but they turned much redder.

9.
This thin fine white linen cloth
must be from Chinan.
I cut and sewed it into a summer jacket,
which shines like figured brocade.

10.
Don't hit the hairpin on my head—
I'm afraid it might fall off.
I fear someone will see
and call me a spinster.

11.
My chest of drawers is filled with clothes,
all adorned with purple thread.
What I most cherish are my childhood clothes—
a pink skirt decorated with lotus flower buds.

12.
Songgŭmdan[218] is best in March,
Kangwŏlsa[219] is perfect in May.
A female peddler of fine-tooth combs from Honan
mistakes my house for a minister's.

---

[218] It seems to be a silk cloth with pine tree patterns, but the details are unknown.
[219] It seems to be a wide silk cloth, but the details are unknown.

13.
I suck the red seeds of ground cherry
until only empty shells are left.
But when I blow the spring wind into the shells,
they swell round again as if filled with seeds.

14.
If Chungbaekki[220] is too sweet, you will tire of it.
I'm afraid that Iganggo[221] might be too strong.
Abalone is the best seafood,
and among fruits June peach is superior.

15.
I stroke the sweet fish-like hair braided behind my ear
and look into the mirror more than a thousand times.
It bothers me that my teeth are too white,
and so I swish light Chinese ink in my mouth.

16.
After getting a tongue lashing from my husband,
I didn't even touch the spoon for three days.
I keep the blue jade bosom knife with me.
Who dares to hurt my feelings?

17.
Peach blossoms look rather cheap,
pear blossoms are cold as frost.
Rouge and powder are perfectly mixed.
I apply apricot makeup.

---

[220] A pastry made of flour dough, seasoned with honey and oil, and fried in oil.
[221] A traditional Korean alcohol made with soju, pear extract, ginger extract, and honey. It is generally regarded as one of three best wines of the Chosŏn period.

18.
My husband likes swallows flying in pairs,
but I like swallows that raise many chicks.
The chicks of one litter are all beautiful.
How can you tell which one was the firstborn?

Libertine Rhymes

The libertine (宕) is what is uncontrollable, deviating from the norm. This section portrays the things of prostitutes. When people's reason and sentiments reach this state, they have deviated too far to ban or regulate. Hence the title of this section, and why there are chŏngp'ung and wip'ung in *The Book of Odes*. It is composed of fifteen poems.

1.
Honey, don't touch my head,
camellia oil may smear your clothes.
Honey, don't get close to my lips,
the sheen of red rouge seems to flow.

2.
My beloved comes smoking cigarettes,
holding a Tongnae tobacco pipe.[222]
I snatch it to hide before he even sits down,
because I love the silver inlaid letters of Life and Blessing.[223]

3.
He snatches my silver ring
and gives me a jade fan weight[224] instead.
He keeps the fan on which Mt. Kŭmgang is painted.
Who will he later give it to?

---

[222] A tobacco pipe produced in Tongnae, South Kyŏngsang Province.
[223] A decoration of the silver-inlaid letters for life 壽 and blessings 福 on a pipe.
[224] A decoration attached to the end of a folding fan.

4.
"Kangsangwŏl[225] in the west pavilion
and Sŏlchungmae[226] in the east tower"—
why did someone take the trouble to write songs
that led me to open my mouth forever?

5.
Honey, don't embrace me—
poverty bothers my head now.
Though I have three thousand pearls,
they are worth only fifteen strings of coin.

6.
When I sing softly in the Kyemyŏn tone,[227]
beating my Dano fan,[228]
those who know me cry,
"Wonderful, wonderful, wonderful."

7.
Though this Ch'uwŏl[229] is old now,
people tried to make me their own, even a few years ago.
What did Mun'gun[230] do for a living?

---

[225] Moon above the river.
[226] Apricot flowers in snow.
[227] One of the tones with which to sing a sijo or a lyric. It provokes sadness.
[228] The fans the king distributes to his subjects and officers on Dano day, when civilians also exchange fans.
[229] A famous gisaeng singer and member of a singing group with vocalist Yi Sech'un and geomungo player Kim Chŏlsŏk, during King Yŏngjo's reign. Here the speaker compares herself to Ch'uwŏl.
[230] Refers to a rich man Zhuo Wangsun's daughter, Zhuo Wenjun. Fascinated by the geomungo sound of Sima Xiangru, she snuck out of her house at midnight and became his wife. They eloped to

I cannot trust her poem.[231]

8.
People try to arrange a match for us,
we are very chaste.
Daily we meet dawn under the lamplight,
among many people.

9.
How can I say his title
when I don't even know his name?
All men with tight sleeves are chiefs of police,
all men in red clothes are high officials.

10.
After I sang Yŏngsan'gok[232]
they made fun of me, calling me "a half-shaman."
Does this mean all the lords and noblemen
sitting here are Hwarangs?[233]

Chengdu; too poor to live there, they moved to Linqiong, where Wenjun sold wine and Xiangru washed dishes.

[231] This seems to refer to an episode in their life. When Sima Xiangru tried to take the daughter of a Maoling as a concubine, Zhuo Wenjun wrote a poem, "Baitouyin" announcing their separation. He abandoned his plan.

[232] A folk song about Bodhisattvas of the vulture peak assembly where Sakyamuni taught.

[233] Hwarang's name derives from the elite youth corps of Silla, but here it refers to groups of entertainers in nice clothes, who were employed to sing and dance.

11.
Chignons of wigs from Yukchin [234]
are decorated with crimson dots.
I make a new karima[235] out of dark blue satin
and wear the wig.

12.
I sing Hujŏnghwa[236] for movement,
and for this piece I have Kŭmgangsan.[237]
Why do you think I'm a musical woman of shamanic rituals?
I have never brought back a grudging spirit to console her.

13.
Petty playboys value gold highly,
while great ones covet fur clothes with blue embroidery.
Is there anyone among the heads of the happy world
who is a clean government officer?

14.
Only Buddhist monks donate money
when I sing Sadangga.[238]
When my voice reaches the climax,
they shout, "Save us, merciful Buddha."[239]

---

[234] High-quality wigs made in Yukchin, one of six military posts in North Hamgyŏng Province.

[235] A dark piece of cloth a woman adds to a wig.

[236] A song title, also called "Pukchŏn." Originally from China, it was sung at the royal court of the Koryŏ dynasty. But in the Chosŏn dynasty it was considered obscene and was rewritten by Sŏnghyŏn to praise the founding of the Chosŏn dynasty.

[237] The title of a court song played in the early Chosŏn period.

[238] A song sung by a wandering troupe.

[239] The literal meaning of the Chinese "Namu Amit'abul" is, in Sanskrit, "Namas Amitabha" (I believe in Amitabha). Amitabha is

15.
T'angp'yŏngch'ae[240] fills the dining table
and Pangmunju[241] soaks in the seats,
while many wives of poor scholars
can't even stuff parched rice into their mouths.

---

the celestial and principle Buddha in Pure Land Buddhism, according to the scriptures of Mahayana Buddhism.
[240] Mung bean jelly salad with vinegar greens added.
[241] White dew wine made of white rice, malt power, and crude spirits.

Unspeakable Rhymes

The Book of Odes says that "'petite graceful rhymes' can be bitter if not yet unspeakable." The unspeakable refers to the bitterness of resentment. Worldly things, in general, slip from the graceful to the beautiful as they slip away from normality; and the beautiful is bound to slip into the libertine—a person bitter with resentment. A really bitter heart will grow abnormal. This is why people write unspeakable rhymes. The unspeakable hates the libertine and seeks the true meaning of gracefulness in reverse, as people think of peace during turmoil. It is composed of sixteen poems.

1.
It's better to be a girl slave in a poor house
than the wife of a petty provincial official.
He comes home when the patrol begins
but leaves as soon as the bell lifting curfew rings.

2.
It's better to be the wife of a petty provincial official
than the wife of a soldier.
Of the three hundred and sixty-five days in a year
you have to spend more than a hundred in an empty room.

3.
It's better to be the wife of a soldier
than the wife of a translator.
The damask and brocade clothes in your chest
cannot match his long absence.

4.
It's better to be the wife of a translator
than the wife of a merchant.

He came back from six months in Honam Province
and departed for Kwansŏ Province this morning.

5.
It's better to be the wife of a merchant
than the wife of a libertine.
I don't know where he wanders in the night,
but he comes home in the morning asking for more wine.

6.
Thinking you manly,
I trusted myself to you.
Why do you abuse me so much
instead of being kind and loving me?

7.
Discovering that the new Sŏksae linen[242] socks I tacked were too wide,
I suddenly lost interest in them.
I should have tailored them
after the pŏsŏn[243] pattern in my chest.

8.
While I was combing my hair,
he took my jade ornamental hairpin.
Useless to have kept it,
but I wonder who he will give it to.

9.
He violently picks up the rice and soup bowls

---

[242] A coarse and thick linen woven with two hundred and forty threads.
[243] Traditional Korean socks.

and hurls them at my face.
Blame it on your changing taste;
my cooking is just the same.

10.
Have the patrols been dismissed?
My husband returns home when the moon sets.
When I fall asleep before him, he gets angry.
When I'm awake, he suspects me.

11.
Raising his long leg,
he kicks me for no reason.
A green bruise grows on my red cheeks—
how can I explain this to my in-laws?

12.
I have long lamented my childlessness,
but it has proved rather good for me.
If my child resembled his father,
I would shed tears for the rest of my life.

13.
A renowned, blind shaman
tells me it is all because of samjae.[244]
I send money to the Bureau of Painting
to buy a picture of a large hawk.

14.
If I see him three thousand times a day
he gets angry three thousand times.

---

[244] Three years of misfortune by fire, water, and wind, as calculated in Korean traditional divinatory practice. It was a custom to paint a three-headed hawk above the door to prevent these disasters.

He will also rag me
for having heels round as eggs.

15.
I kept the old red skirt from my wedding
to sew into my shroud.
And when I sold it this morning
to pay my husband's debts, I wept.

16.
Drawing water from the well under the zelkova tree,
I was struck by a painful thought:
if I divorce and live alone, my body will be comfortable,
but my in-laws will still live in that house.

Stories

The Story of Student Sim

Student Sim, a nobleman from Seoul, is twenty years old, handsome and elegant.

On his way home from watching the royal procession on Unjong Street[245] he saw a stout maid servant carrying on her back a woman covered in purple silk, trailed by a girl holding red silk shoes. Judging from her size, he assumed the woman was not a child.

He followed close behind, his sleeve brushing against them, but he never took his eyes off the silk cloth. When they arrived at the Sokwangt'ong Bridge, a whirlwind blew, unfurling the purple cloth. Wow, it was a lady, with peach-colored cheeks and willow leaf-like eyebrows, wearing a green jacket and a scarlet skirt. There was beautiful powder and rouge on her face. Even at a glance he knew she was a matchless beauty. She also noticed, vaguely, through the cloth, a handsome boy wearing a straw hat and indigo cloth following them on their right and then their left. Just in time she made eyes at him through a chink in the cloth.

When the cloth was blown off, their four eyes—two willow eyes and two stars—struck each other. Surprised and ashamed, she drew the cloth over her and hurried away. How could Mr. Sim lose this opportunity? He chased after them and saw the lady disappear through the second gate, when they arrived at the red gate with a spiked top in Sogongju-dong.

As if he had lost something, he wandered in a daze. Then he met an old woman living nearby and asked after the lady. She told him the house belonged to a retired accountant from the Ministry of Finance; the couple had a daughter of sixteen or seventeen years old, but they hadn't decided whom she

---

[245] Present-day Chongno Street in downtown Seoul.

should marry. He asked where she lived. She pointed in that direction.

"If you turn at this crossroads," she said, "you'll see a lime-washed wall. She lives in a small room inside that wall."

Mr. Sim couldn't erase her words from his mind, so he lied to his family that evening.

"A friend of mine wants to spend the night with me, and I'd like to go out."

He waited until there were no passersby before climbing over the wall. Light from the crescent moon was dim, but he could see that the trees and flowers outside the window were neatly kept—the lamp shone brightly through the rice paper window. He sat against the wall under the eaves to wait, holding his breath.

In the room were two handmaids and the lady. She was reading a novel written in the Korean alphabet in a low voice, which sounded like the song of an oriole chick. Her maid fell into a sound sleep by midnight, when she finally put out the lamp and went to bed. But she didn't fall asleep for a while and seemed to be worried, tossing and turning.

It was impossible for Mr. Sim to feel sleepy or to stir. He stayed there until the daybreak bell rang and then climbed back over the wall again.

It became his routine to go there at night and return at dawn. This continued for twenty days, but he never tired. She would read novels and sew clothes in the evening and put out the lamp around midnight. Sometimes she fell asleep right away but some nights she was too anxious to sleep. After a week, she said she didn't feel well and fell onto her pillow early in the evening. Again and again she would strike the wall with her hands and exhale long sighs and groans loud enough to be heard outside. This grew worse by the day.

It was the twentieth evening when the lady suddenly walked out the door and around the outside wall to where Mr.

Sim was sitting. He sprang up in the jet-black darkness and grabbed her. Without any show of surprise, she told him in a hushed voice, "You must be the person I met at the Sokwangt'ong Bridge? For the last twenty days, I knew you were coming to this place. Please let me go free. If I scream, you'll never walk out of here. If you release me, I will open the back door and let you come into my room. Please!"

Believing her, he let her go and waited. She rounded the wall slowly to enter her room, where she called her maid. "Go ask my mother to give me the big tin lock. It's really dark tonight, and I'm afraid someone might sneak in."

The maid went to the upper room and soon came back with the lock. The lady latched the back doorknob she had promised to open and fastened the lock, with a loud clink. Then she put out the lamp light and pretended to sleep, though in reality she couldn't fall asleep.

Deceived, Mr. Sim was infuriated, but he consoled himself with the thought that he saw her anyway. He spent the night outside her locked door and returned home at dawn.

He came back the next day and the day after. Undaunted, though the door was locked, he wore an oilpaper raincoat when it rained and didn't care even when his clothes were wet. Ten more days passed like this. At midnight, when all the people in the house fell into a sound sleep, she put out the lamp but after a while she suddenly stood up, called her maids, and ordered them to turn on the lamp. "You girls, go and sleep in the upper room tonight."

After they left, she unlocked the door with the key hanging on the wall, and called out, "Young gentleman, please come in." He found himself in the room in the blink of an eye. She locked the door again and said, "Please sit down here and wait"

Then she went to the upper room and returned with her parents. They were surprised when they saw him. She said, "Don't be startled but listen to me. I'm seventeen years old and

I have never stepped outside the house gate. But a month ago on my way home from watching the royal procession the cloth covering me blew off, and I met a young man wearing a straw hat. Since that night, he has not missed a day for thirty days in a row to come and hide under this door. He came when it rained, when it was cold, and even when I refused him by locking the door. I have thought the matter over. If a rumor of someone coming at evening and departing at dawn spreads to the neighbors, who would believe he had sat outside the window alone? I will be falsely accused, and my fate will be that of a pheasant bitten by a dog. The young man is a descendant of a noble family and is in his prime youth when passion cannot be controlled. He only knows how to covet flowers like bees and butterflies but doesn't care whether or not he is exposed to the wind and dew. Surely he will fall sick within days. If he is taken by illness, I'm certain he will never recover. In which case I will be blamed for his death, though I'm innocent. Even if no one knows the facts, karma will follow me. I'm just the daughter of a bureaucratic middle-class family. I'm not a marvel of beauty before whom fish hide themselves and flowers feel ashamed, but he takes a kite for a falcon and steadfastly devotes his heart and soul to me. If I don't accept him, heaven will hate me and grant me no blessing. I've made up my mind. Dear parents, please don't worry. Because you're old and I have no brothers or sisters, I think I should find a husband who will live with my family. Supporting my parents while they're alive and performing ancestral rites when they're dead were all I ever wished for. Unexpectedly, things went this way, but I think this is also the will of heaven. What use is there in saying more?

Her bewildered parents said nothing, nor could Mr. Sim speak. He and the lady were finally able to sleep together. Their joy, after so much longing and yearning, was beyond expression. After that night, he never failed to go out in the evening and return home at dawn.

Her family was rich, so they made a nice dress for him. But he couldn't wear it in his home for fear his family might think it strange. He was careful, but his family couldn't help wondering why he went out at night and didn't return until morning. Eventually, they ordered him to go to a Buddhist temple to study. This made him very unhappy, but under pressure from his family and led by his friends, he went up to the Pukhan Fortress with a bundle of books.

After a month had passed in the Zen temple, he received a letter from the lady written in the Korean alphabet informing him of her eternal separation. She had passed away. The contents of her letter went roughly like this: The spring days are still cold. How are your studies going in the temple? I miss you, and not a day goes by without me thinking of you. After you left, I fell into a sickness, which no drug can cure. Now I know there is no future for me except death. What use can there be for such a star-crossed woman like me to survive? But I cannot close my eyes before my looming death because I have three big regrets in my heart.

As an only child, I received enough love. My parents hoped to find a suitable son-in-law and rely on him in later life. As you say that good comes with bad, they met an unexpected fate: a creeper clung to the tall pine tree presumptuously, but their marriage is expected to end soon. Without any pleasure, I suffered many anxieties and now face death by disease. My old parents have no one to rely on. This is my first regret.

Once a woman leaves her house for marriage, even if she is a slave she will have her husband and in-laws unless she is a street walker who stands against the door and waits for her customers. Is there any daughter-in-law who doesn't know her in-laws? I have been cheated, I haven't seen the old female slave in your house for months. I'm leaving dishonorable traces in this life and will become a wandering ghost after death. This is my second regret.

When a wife serves her husband, nothing is greater than preparing his food and sewing his clothes. Many days have passed since we met, during which I sewed clothes for you. But you haven't eaten a meal or worn a suit in my house. I served you only in bed. This is my third regret.

Shortly after we met, we were forced to separate forever, I got sick, and now I face death. It is a sorrow for a woman like me that I cannot bid you farewell. How can I dare to tell this to a gentleman like you? When my thoughts go there, it feels as if my bowels have been sliced up and my bones dissolved. Though the fragile grass is flattened by the wind and petals turn into dust, I wonder when my regrets will end.

Now our secret meeting by the window is over. I hope you don't keep me in your thoughts but devote yourself to your studies and achieve your dreams. I pray that you keep your health.

Mr. Sim wept reading her letter. But what use is crying now? He threw away his brushes to become a military officer and was promoted to Director of the Internal Security Division. But he also died young.

The unauthorized historian of Maehwa-dong writes:

When I was twelve, I studied in the village school with my friends and daily enjoyed hearing stories. One day, my teacher told us Student Sim's story: "Mr. Sim was my colleague when we were young. I was there when he received the letter and wailed in the temple. That's why I still remember the story." He added, "I don't mean that you should follow the example of this elegant gentleman. If one determines to do something, he can move even a lady in her boudoir. So you have no reason not to finish your studies and pass the national exams."

Hearing this story at the time, we thought it was new. But when I later read *Chŏngsa*,²⁴⁶ I found many similar stories. I add this one as a supplement to the book.

---

²⁴⁶ 情史, *The History of Amours Affairs*, edited by Feng Meng Ming, 馮夢龍 (1574-1646), also called 情史類略 or 情天寶鑑, is made up of twenty-four volumes with eight hundred and sixty works.

The Story of Song Silsol,[247] a Singer

Silsol, a singer from Seoul, earned his name because he was so good at singing "Song of Silsol."[248]

He learned to sing in his youth. When he finally learned how to project his voice, he went daily to sing by a loud waterfall. Almost a year passed before the sound of the waterfall could no longer be heard; only his song remained. He also climbed to the top of Pugak Mountain to sing wildly to the sky; at first his singing dispersed in the air, but after a year a storm could not scatter his voice.

Since then, when he sang in his room, the sound rang in the crossbeams; when he sang on the wooden floor, it rang in the front gate. When he sang in the boat, it rang in the mast; when he sang by a stream or in the forest, it rang among the clouds. His singing was strong as the sound of a gong, clear as a jade ball, feeble as fluttering smoke, remaining firm as a unmoving cloud, enchanting as orioles in their prime, bursting open like the roar of a dragon. His singing went nicely with the sounds of kŏmun'go,[249] saenghwang,[250] t'ungso,[251] and chaeng,[252] which made the most delicate harmonies. When he wore a gat[253] and dressed up to sing in front of a crowd, everyone listened carefully and gazed absently at the sky, not knowing who was singing.

---

[247] Details about him are unknown. He was one of the famous singers of his time, along with Yi Sech'un and Chi Pongsŏ (their names appear in *Popular Songs of the East* and *Ancient and Modern Singers*) as indicated in this story.

[248] Silsol is a cricket; hence "The Song of a Cricket."

[249] A Korean musical instrument with six strings, similar to a zither.

[250] A reed instrument with a number of pipes of different lengths.

[251] A six-holed bamboo flute.

[252] A musical instrument with thirteen strings.

[253] A traditional Korean hat made of bamboo and horsehair.

At that time, Prince Sŏp'yŏng—Yi P'yo, a royal descendant—was rich and gallant and loved music. Silsol's song delighted him, and he went around with him every day. Whenever Silsol sang, the Prince accompanied him on the kŏmun'go. He was also a renowned player of the kŏmun'go, and so their meetings were always pleasant.

The Prince once asked Silsol, "Can you sing a song I cannot accompany on kŏmun'go?"

Silsol sang "Ch'wisŭnggok"[254] in the hujŏnghwa[255] tone, elongating his sounds. The song goes like this:

I cut up a monk's robe to sew underwear for a beautiful woman,
and cut open a Buddhist rosary to make a bridle for a donkey.
Ten years of studying were for nothing.
Where will I live hereafter? Let's go that way.

When the song turned to Act 3, he shouted "Tang," the sound of a monk's para.[256] The Prince hurried to take out the plectrum and struck the body of the kŏmun'go in

---

[254] A song parodying a drunken Buddhist monk. The lyric is recorded in various anthologies of songs, including *Songs of the Green Hills* compiled by Kim Ch'ŏnt'aek.
[255] Originally it was "The Jade Tree Behind the Garden Flower," a sad song written by Houzhu of Chen. There seemed to be a song called "Hujŏnghwa" at the time of Song Silsol.
[256] The small gong used in Buddhist ceremonies.

accompaniment. Silsol changed his tone to "Naksijo"[257] and sang "Hwanggyegok."[258] It goes like this:

> Let's play until the yellow cock
> painted on the wall cranes his long neck,
> claps two wings, and crows.

After imitating the sound of a cock dragging its tail, Silsol laughed heartily. The Prince played the "kung note" and the "kak note"[259] before he dropped his plectrum, unable to find the right harmony. "I couldn't follow you," he said. "Why did you first make a bara sound then laugh?"

Silsol replied, "When a monk chants a sutra, he always ends by striking a para. And when a cock stops crowing, it always sounds like a laugh. That's why I did it."

The Prince and many others laughed. Silsol's humor was like that. The Prince liked music so much that many famous singers of the day, including Yi Sech'un, Cho Oja, Chi Pongsŏ, and Pak Sech'ŏm, gathered under his patronage and got along well with Silsol. When Sech'un's mother died, Silsol and his company visited Sech'un's house to pay condolences. Crossing the threshold, he heard the chief mourner crying and said,

---

[257] A tune for singing sijos. Originally it meant "a low tone" but it grew into the tune singing chain sijos during the reigns of King Yŏngjo and Chŏngjo.

[258] A song inviting people to give themselves over to pleasure. The lyrics are recorded in many anthologies, including *Songs of the Green Hills* compiled by Kim Ch'ŏntaek.

[259] Kung, Sang, Kak, Ch'i, and U (do, re, mi, sol, la) are the five notes in Oriental music.

"That is a kemyŏn tone.[260] It should be a p'yŏng and a u tone."[261]

He approached the dead woman and wailed, and his wailing sounded like music. Those who heard him relayed the story with a laugh.

The Prince kept a dozen private servants who played musical instruments, and all the women he supported were also fine singers and dancers. He passed away after playing music and enjoying every pleasure for twenty years. Silsol and his company met ruin, grew old, and died. Now only Pak Sech'ŏm lived with a woman, Maewŏl, under Pugak Mountain. He was often drunk, and when he stopped singing he would talk about the Prince and their happy times, crying helplessly.

---

[260] A sad and melancholy tone in traditional Korean music.
[261] A combination of the p'yŏng tone and the u tone, which has a low, grand tone.

The Story of Ryu Kwang'ŏk

The whole world simmers with the pursuit of money; everyone seeks it. The world has long worshipped money. But he who lives for money is destined to die for it. Therefore noblemen do not talk about money, but ordinary people die for it.

Seoul is a place where poor craftsmen and merchants gather. Stores with all sorts of goods to buy and sell are scattered about like stars, spreading like a go game board. One sells one's own hands and fingers, one sells one's shoulders and back, one cleans another's toilets, one hones a knife to butcher cows, one decorates one's face to prostitute oneself. In this world, the business of selling and buying has reached its summit.

Mr. Oesa[262] says, "No markets sold threads and silk in the country of naked people, and no pots were sold when people hunted animals and ate them uncooked. Only when there is a need does a seller appear. No one advertises a knife or hammer by the blacksmith's door; the rice peddler stops shouting when he passes a diligent farmer's house. People seek from others what they do not have."

Ryu Kwang'ŏk was from Hapch'ŏn County in Yŏngnam Province. He had some skill in writing poetry, and it was said he did well in poetry composition on the state examination in the southern provinces. But he was of a lower class and his family was poor. Many people made a living selling writings for the state examination, according to the country custom, and Ryu also did that for his own profit. He passed the Yŏngnam Province local examination and was on his way to Seoul to take the state exam when he was greeted by some people who had brought a wagon for a woman. When he arrived, he saw red gates one after another and dozens of magnificent houses. A

---

[262] Literally, "unofficial historian." This refers to the writer himself.

few pale people with sparse beards were spreading papers, writing, boasting of their skill, awaiting instructions to go forward or back. The owner of the house lodged Ryu in the main building and provided five sumptuous meals a day. He visited Ryu three or four times a day, treating him tenderly, like a son supporting his parents. Finally the state exam came, and the son of the house passed the exam with Ryu's writing to become a chinsa.[263] The owner sent Ryu home with lots of luggage, and he returned with a horse and servant to find he also had twenty thousand chŏns,[264] and the grain he had borrowed from the local government had been paid off by the provincial governor.

Ryu's diction was not high, but he was clever, and his writing prospered in the state exam; his fame grew nationwide.

When the officer of the exam met the provincial governor, he asked, "Who is the most talented man in Yŏngnam Province?"

The governor replied, "A man named Ryu Kwang'ŏk."

"I will surely award him first-place this time."

"Can you pick him out?"

"Certainly."

They argued about whether he could pick out Ryu's writing and finally agreed to make a bet. The officer went to the exam site and announced the subject for poetry writing, "We have the Double Nine Festival[265] in October in Yŏngnam, but it saddens us that the weather in the south and the north are different." After a while, a poem was submitted:

> The double yang festival is held in the double yin month.

---

[263] Someone who has passed the first examination for office.
[264] Chŏn was a unit of money in the Chosŏn period.
[265] The festival held on the ninth day of the ninth month on the lunar calendar. On this seasonal holiday, people write poems and eat chrysanthemum pancakes.

The northern guest, forced to drink the heated liquor of the south, got tipsy.

Reading this, the officer said, "This has Ryu's flair."
He placed pijŏms[266] on it with red ink, graded it iha,[267] and selected it as a winner. He selected another poem for its remarkable technique, then another, and then he opened the sealed edge of the papers to check the names: no Ryu. But a secret investigation revealed that he had written all three poems, distributing them according to what he was paid for each. When the officer learned this, he feared the provincial governor would not trust him to evaluate poetry. He sent a warrant for Ryo's arrest to Hapch'ŏn County in order to secure from him a statement, which he could use as evidence, though he did not intend to jail him.

Ryu was seized with fear even before the governor had him arrested. "I am a thief in the state examination," he said. "If I go there, I will surely be put to death. So it is better not to go." After drinking heavily with his relatives, he drowned himself in the river. Hearing this, the examiner felt sorry for him. Everyone pitied the loss of such a talent, but the nobleman said, "It is right that he should be put death and be gone."

Maehwaoesa[268] wrote:

Nothing in the world cannot be sold. You can sell your body to become another's slave, you can buy and sell minute hairs and even dreams with no substance. But no one can sell

---

[266] Pijŏm is a round dot that evaluators and examiners place on fine sentences and poems.
[267] Among the grades given for poetry writing, this is the third one in the second rating.
[268] Another penname of Yi Ok.

his heart. Is it because one can sell everything but one's heart? Was Ryu someone who sold even his heart? Ah, who could imagine that a man of letters made the most ignoble trade of all tradable things? The Book of Law says, "To give and to receive are the same crime."

The Story of Chang Pokson

We have known in our history many chivalrous figures—people who loitered in pleasure quarters and entrusted their bodies to the sword, like Ch'ŏngnŭnggye.[269] Or those who drank and played mah-jong, without taking care of their household. But were they true fighters?

More recently, Talmun [270] earned a reputation as a chivalrous fighter in Seoul. At fifty, he was still unmarried and dressed shabbily, though he made friends with the rich in their silks, calling them brothers. When in his youth he played at a friend's house, a bag of silver vanished. The friend suspected Talmun. "Did you see the silver here?" he said.

"Yes, I saw it there."

Talmun apologized for taking it without telling him. He borrowed silver from someone else and gave it to his friend, who subsequently found the lost silver in his house. Ashamed, he returned the other silver to Talmun, apologizing profusely. Talmun said with a smile, "It's ok. You found your silver, and I got mine back. Why should you apologize?"

Thus his name became known to the world.

Kyŏnggŭmja[271] said, "Ku Talmun isn't chivalrous, just a gentleman from a residential district. For the chivalrous do not dwell on making money but help others, respect the spirit of chivalry, and take care of others' needs without expectation of repayment. Isn't this true chivalry?"

Chang Pokson was a keeper of silver in the P'yŏngyang provincial administration.

---

[269] Details about him are unknown.
[270] A famous chivalrous fighter working in the streets of Seoul during the reign of Yŏngjo, he was also known as Kwangmun.
[271] Yi Ok's penname.

When Minister Ch'aejegong was Governor of P'yŏng'an Province, he checked the warehouse and discovered that two thousand nyangs of silver were missing. Poksŏn was too poor to collect silver from, and so the governor was legally bound to sentence him to death the next day. All the people in P'yŏngyang felt sorry for him, and a rumor reached the governor that they were rushing to bring food and liquor to the prison.

At midnight, Minister Ch'ae sent his man to check on Poksŏn, who was holding a glass, calmly conversing with his friends. Suddenly he asked for a brush and paper.

"I don't feel too bad that I have to die," he said. "But it's shameful to hear I stole government property for myself. Thus I will leave a document to prove my innocence."

Then he wrote: "When a certain person was too poor to clean and shroud a corpse at a funeral, I gave him some nyangs of silver. I gave more nyangs of silver for another funeral. I sponsored a girl to be married, and I spent a few nyangs of silver to marry off a bachelor. I used some nyangs of silver to pay off someone's grain loan and a petty official's embezzlement."

When he finished adding it up, it came to more than two thousand nyangs.

The next morning, flags were raised to announce the verdict, and Poksŏn was forced to his knees. The execution was almost at hand when the people of P'yŏngyang ran here and there, saying to one another, "Petty official Chang Poksŏn will be executed today." Men and women of all ages circled around to watch, some shedding tears. About a hundred gisaengs, with braided hairpieces and their long silk skirts rolled up and tucked into their belts, knelt down in rows in front of the prison yard and sang to one another:

Please save that man, save that man,

Chang Poksŏn, we pray tens of thousands of times.
Minister Ch'ae from Mi-dong,
Please save Chang Pokson.
If you save him,
You will be promoted to chancellor.
Otherwise you will have a second son
Who wears a long, thin silk hair ribbon.
Please save that man, save that man, we pray and pray
That you save Chang Pokson and let him live out his allotted span of life.

Before the song ended, a military officer put down his big wicker baskets and shouted, "Today, Chang Pokson will die. If you want to save his life, please chip in your silver here."

Because P'yŏng'an Province was blessed with silver deposits and luxury was general, everyone had some sort of silver decoration. They threw in silver bosom knives, long silver hairpins, women's rings, hairpins, norigaes.[272] They fell like snow, filling four or five baskets in no time, which a petty official measured as weighing one thousand nyangs. Minister Ch'ae, listening to the people and admiring Pokson's humanity, donated five hundred nyangs of silver and ordered Pokson's release. The next day the government ledger was reported fully restored.

Three days after Pokson's release, two or three people arrived with silver in carts from distant towns. They were happy to hear the news but ashamed for arriving late.

Kyŏnggŭmja says, "Someone like Chang Pokson is truly a chivalrous fighter. Because he nibbled away at government property while privately helping others, he surely deserves death, according to the law. But was he guilty of a crime, even

---

[272] Woman's clothing ornament or pendant.

if money was found in his house? Because our people are dull, narrow-minded, and stingy, few help others in trouble. Though he was a petty official, he acted like a great chivalrous man. Is this because Kwansŏ Province has different morals and customs? They praise fidelity, not money, value unyielding spirit and integrity, respect honor."

Not long ago, a traveler passing through P'yŏngyang asked after Chang Poksŏn, only to learn that he had gone to Anju and never returned.

The Story of Yi Hong

People were simpler in the old days, but nowadays people respect wit. Wit gives birth to skill, skill to craft, and craft to trickery. When trickery runs rampant, morality deteriorates by the day.

There is a big market at Sŏdaemun in Seoul, a den of dealers in counterfeit goods. They insist nickel is silver, goat horn is tortoiseshell, and dog hide, marten hide. Father and son or brothers pretend to bargain, noisily arguing over prices. If a country person, watching this, pays the asking price, thinking he is buying something genuine, the seller earns anywhere from ten to a hundred times as much. And there are pickpockets who cut open sacks or purses with a sharp knife and remove what's inside. The victim chasing the pickpocket runs this way and that into a narrow, winding alley, where sweet rice drinks are sold. When he almost catches up to the pickpocket, a young man with a huge bamboo basket rushes out shouting "Baskets!" and blocks the road. The pickpocket escapes. People often fall for this, even if they guard their money like a battlefield camp and watch their goods like a bride taking care of her body.

The people of the Three Hans[273] were called simple, but nowadays some are notorious fraudsters like Paek Myŏnsŏn.[274] Is this because their customs were corrupted day by day and the simple turned sly? Were there also cunning people in the ancient, ignorant world?

Yi Hong lived in Seoul. With his fine appearance and silver tongue, strangers didn't know he was a swindler. He put on a good show with his fine clothes and food, but he was poor.

At an early age, Hong frequented the houses of mighty families and authorities, talking about water management.

---

[273] Refers to the ancient Three States of Mahan, Pyŏnhan, and Chinhan.
[274] Details about him remain unknown.

After cadging ten thousand nyangs from them, he worked in construction by the Ch'ŏngch'ŏn River, daily he butchered cows and strained liquor, and invited famous gisaengs from near and far; none refused him. But he couldn't get one gisaeng in Anju, whose wit and beauty were second to none in P'yŏng'an Province. She was also a favorite of the governor. Even the king's envoy couldn't peek at her face.

Hong bet his friends he would go to Anju and bring her back within ten days. He loaded his luggage on a horse and, wearing silk kwaeja,[275] cracked his whip all the way to Anju fortress, accompanied not by a kujong,[276] but a man with a horsehair hat. Anyone with good sense would have recognized him as "a great merchant of Kaesŏng."

Hong went to the gisaeng's house and lodged there. Her father was a military cadre who in old age had opened a tavern. Hong said, "What I have is very precious. Please don't admit any other guests. I have to wait for someone, but I don't know whether he will arrive sooner or later. I'll pay all my bills when I leave. I'm a picky eater, so please prepare my meals carefully. Don't worry about the price. You can set it."

The gisaeng's father took him for a merchant—his bags were heavy with what looked like silver coins.

"Wow, he must be a good guest."

He cleaned his private room and welcomed him. Hong looked at the room, frowned, and called his servant. "Buy thick, strong paper. How can someone like me stay in a room like this even for a day?"

After hanging new wallpaper, he moved his luggage by his bed, spread a wool mattress and silk blanket, then took from his bag a thick ledger book, an abacus, and a small ink stone. After locking the door, he seemed to spend the day doing

---

[275] A sleeveless military uniform with an open seam in the back.
[276] A servant to a government official.

accounts with his servant. When the gisaeng's father eavesdropped through the hole in the door, he heard them calculating amounts of silk, spices, and medicinal herbs. He said to his wife, a retired gisaeng, "This guest is a businessman. If he sees our daughter, he will surely have a crush on her. That will be good for us, too. This will not compare to the governor's favor."

They called their daughter home secretly from the P'yŏngyang provincial administration and let her bow to him at his door.

"Because an honored guest is staying long at my humble house, my young lady will dare show herself to you."

Hong, pretending to be busy, said, "You don't have to do that."

Flicking the abacus beads, he seemed not to care a fig for her. Her father said to himself, "That man is truly a great businessman. He behaves like this because of his discernment and enormous wealth." He talked again to Hong quietly that evening.

"Is my daughter not fair enough for you? You're so cold to her, and she lives in shame."

But Hong still showed no interest, though later he reluctantly relented. The gisaeng brought a liquor table, sang and danced suggestively with him, and then, as luck would have it, she slept with him. Afterwards, she stayed with him for three or four days.

One day, Hong knitted his brows and called the landlord with an anxious look. "Did bright anger bandits appear at Sŏdo?"[277]

"No."

"How many days does it take to travel from Ŭiju to here?"

"A few days."

---

[277] Refers to Hwanghae Province and P'yŏng'an Province.

"Then the date is already past. Did the horses fall sick?"

"Dear guest, is there anything that upsets you?"

"The goods coming from Yanjing were supposed to cross the Yalu River and arrive here on a certain day. But they haven't arrived yet. That bothers me."

He ordered his servant to the West Gate to watch. The servant returned that evening to report there was no news.

Hong spent two days worrying, and on the third day he called on the landlord. "I have precious things with me, so I cannot go outside. But now you are as intimate as family. I feel stuffed up and fear I may fall ill. I cannot sit and wait any longer. I trust my luggage to you, please take good care of it. I will go out to check and come back."

Hong locked his room and went out, taking a byway to return to the Ch'ŏngch'ŏn River. It took just ten days as he promised.

At the gisaeng's house, they felt weird about the guest not returning for so long and opened the luggage. Inside were pebbles the size of goose eggs.

A provincial petty official came to Seoul with a thousand strings of coins to pay the military clothing tax. Seeing he had not decided where to stay, Hong took him to his house to trick him. "I have an idea," he said. "You can earn money to cover your travel, or you can visit a prostitute."

Pleased with this idea, the official entrusted his money to Hong, who seemed to earn money morning and night. Ten days passed. Hong suddenly praised the beauty of Namsan Mountain. Clutching a bottle of liquor, he made the petty official go ahead and climb to a desolate place in the P'aengnam valley. Hong finished off the bottle and cried bitterly.

"Can't you bear just a bottle of liquor? Why are you crying?"

"Oh, I have to leave Seoul when it is so beautiful! How can I not cry?"

He looped a rope over a pine bough and tried to hang himself.

Astonished, the petty official stopped him and asked him why he was doing this.

"It's because of you," said Hong. "Would I cheat someone? Falsely trusting somebody, I was robbed of all your money. I'd like to pay you back, but I am too poor. And I can't leave it as it is, because you will press me to pay you back. It's better to die. Please don't stop me."

He prepared to jump, with the rope around his neck. The petty official was so perplexed he stood on tiptoe and said, "Don't kill yourself. I won't say another word about the money."

"No, you are saying that because I'm about to jump. But words are not a document. How can I protect myself from your accusation? Better to kill myself now."

The official thought to himself, "I won't get my money back, whether he lives or dies. But people will talk if he dies." He hastily took his brush and ink from his pocket and wrote a certificate that he had received the money, while persuading him not to kill himself.

"When you treat me so ardently, I have no reason to die."

After shaking the dust off his clothes, Hong returned home. That evening he drove the petty official away and never again allowed him to cross the gate of his house.

When the judge heard this, he had Hong lashed a hundred times, and he nearly died.

Hong learned how to shoot a bow and arrow, but it was not for his archery score that he passed the military exam. When the roster of successful candidates was posted, Hong held the most extravagant yuga[278] ceremony. All court musicians wore blue linen coats with pleats and three cha of hanging aloe-wood threads. He gave them not only a towel, money, and cloth but also a set of folding screens of peony and an encased ornamental knife with an oxhorn handle decorated with grapes. People said Hong traveled to distant places, weeded many graves on behalf of others, and spent the money he earned from selling their chewijŏns.[279]

Hong's house was located outside Sŏdaemun Gate. One day, he loitered by Namdaemun Gate in a light, flower-patterned overcoat, touching with his left hand the manho hat string and rolling the weight of his folding fan with his right.[280] A Buddhist monk was asking for alms, striking kyŏngsoe.[281]

Hong called to the monk. "How long have you been standing here?"

"Three days."

"How much have you earned?"

"Only about two hundred puns."[282]

"Alas, you'll grow old and die doing this. Only two hundred puns in three days, chanting 'Namuamit'abul.'[283] I'm rich with many children. I always wanted to do good for the Buddha. Today you are blessed. What can I give you as an offering?" Hong gave himself over to thought and then said, "I have some brassware. Is that of any use to you?"

---

[278] The ritual in which a successful candidate on the state exam parades through the streets with musicians, visiting his mentors, previous successful candidates, and relatives.

[279] A paddy field dedicated to ancestral rituals; produce from the field was used to pay for its upkeep.

[280] A rough horsehair hat string with no discernable pattern.

[281] A musical instrument made of stone or jade.

[282] A pun is a Korean penny.

[283] "Save us, merciful Buddha," one of the most common Buddhist chants.

"No charity is greater than making a statue of Buddha with brass."

"Please follow me."

Hong went to Namdaemun Gate and, pointing to a lighted house, said, "Let's rest there."

The mistress of the tavern warmed liquor and brought them various relishes. Hong drank down a dozen cups and laughed heartily, touching his silk pocket,

"I forgot to bring my purse when I left home today. Can I borrow the money in your knapsack? I'll pay you back as soon as I get home."

The monk paid the bill. They left the tavern, and Hong said to him, "Are you following me?"

"Yes, of course."

"The brassware is old. People may block you. You must be careful with it."

"Donating it is on you. Bringing it is on me. Do you think I can't do this?"

"No."

They went into another tavern and drank with the monk's money. When they had done this three or four times, the monk's money was gone.

Hong walked on, saying to the monk. "People should be sensible about everything."

"This poor monk has lived his whole life that way. Sensibility is all I have."

"Is that so?" said Hong. He took a few more steps, turned around, and said, "This brassware is really big. With what power can you carry it?"

"The bigger, the better. If you give it to me, even ten thousand geun[284] will be no problem for me."

"Ok, then."

---

[284] A Korean unit of weight, about six hundred grams.

Now they passed Taekwangt'onggyo Bridge.[285] Turning onto the eastern road, Hong raised his fan high and pointed at the Injŏng bell[286] in the belfry.

"The brassware is there. You should take it carefully." The monk stood upright, blankly staring at Namsan Mountain, then ran away.

Hong loitered by Ch'ŏlchŏn Bridge.[287] Yi Hong's life was like this, these stories being the most notorious. He was famous for cheating people, and then the government exiled him.

Mr. Oesa says, "A great fraud cheats the whole world, a lesser fraud cheats the king and his ministers, and a still lesser fraud cheats the people. Yi Hong's low-class fraud does not merit discussion. But he who cheats the whole world becomes a king, the next one glorifies his body, and the next one makes his family rich. Yi Hong was finally caught in the net of law because of his fraud; in fact he did not cheat others but only himself. This is sad indeed.

---

[285] The longest bridge over the Ch'ŏnggyech'ŏn stream in Seoul.
[286] The bell in the Posin'gak in Chongno, Seoul. The original bell was 3.18m high, 2.28 in diameter, and weighed 19.96 tons. The current bell is a replica of the original.
[287] The bridge located at Kwanch'ŏl-dong.

About the Translators

Won-Chung Kim is a professor of English Literature at Sungkyunkwan University in Seoul, Korea, where he teaches contemporary American poetry, ecological literature, and translation. He has translated fourteen books of Korean poetry into English, including *Because of the Rain: A Selection of Korean Zen Poems* and Seungja Choi's *Phone Bells Keep Ringing for Me* (2021 National Translation Award Long List). He has also translated John Muir's *My First Summer in the Sierra* and H. D. Thoreau's *Natural History Essays* into Korean.

Christopher Merrill has published eight collections of poetry, including *Watch Fire*, for which he received the Lavan Younger Poets Award from the Academy of American Poets; many edited volumes and translations; and six books of nonfiction, among them, *Only the Nails Remain: Scenes from the Balkan Wars, Things of the Hidden God: Journey to the Holy Mountain, The Tree of the Doves: Ceremony, Expedition, War*, and *Self-Portrait with Dogwood*. He directs the International Writing Program at the University of Iowa.

Hyeonwu Lee received her Ph.D. from Sungkyunkwan University, where she studied classical Korean literature with a dissertation titled "A Study of the Sketch Prose of Yi Ok." She has taught at many universities, including Sungkyunkwan University, and worked as a researcher at Sungkyunkwan University's Center for Humanities and a research professor at Dongguk University's Center for the Cultural Studies. A specialist in classical Korean literature written in Chinese characters, she has translated many classical writers into modern Korean.

Milton Keynes UK
Ingram Content Group UK Ltd.
UKHW030632071024
449371UK00001B/131